NEW INTERNATIONAL VERSION
Bible Guide

KU-175-287

NEW INTERNATIONAL VERSION

Bible Guide

Edited by
Elizabeth Heike
and
Peter Toon

HODDER & STOUGHTON
LONDON SYDNEY AUCKLAND TORONTO

British Library Cataloguing in Publication Data

Bible guide.
  1. Bible. Interpretation
  I. Heike, Elizabeth   II. Toon, Peter
  220.6

  ISBN 0-340-50170-7

CONTENTS

LIST OF TABLES

THE REV'D DR PETER TOON is the vicar of Staindrop, County Durham and the author/editor of many books. He is a part-time visiting lecturer at colleges in this country and overseas and a member of the Advisory Board of the C S Lewis Centre.

ELIZABETH HEIKE is a Course Tutor in the External Studies Department of the London Bible College. She is the author of *A Question of Grief*, and a member of St Andrew's Church, Chorleywood.

INTRODUCTION

HOW TO USE THE BIBLE GUIDE

This guide is intended to help you to study and understand your Bible. You will want to refer to it from time to time whenever you study the Bible and although it cannot possibly tell you all you want to know, it will provide you with a lot of background information.

First, a word about using Bible references. What does 1 Corinthians 1:18 mean? If you look at the contents page of your Bible you will see the books of the Bible listed. Notice that several books have two parts: Samuel and Kings in the Old Testament for example. Corinthians is in the New Testament and so our reference is to the first book of Corinthians. After the name of the book comes the chapter of the book and then the verse—in this case, chapter one, verse eighteen.

The first section includes tables and background information. You will see that some words are printed in bold type and this should help you to see quickly what is covered in each paragraph. Some words have an asterisk beside them which indicates that they are more fully explained in the Bible Index. Sometimes though, a word is explained in more detail in the first section. For example, 'law' has a longer paragraph here than in the Bible Index. Remember, this section cannot give you all the information you might need. It is an introduction to help you get started.

Next there are several maps which show the countries mentioned in the Bible as well as particular periods of Bible history. For example, there is a map showing the places connected with the life of Jesus.

Finally, the Bible Index is arranged for use as a dictionary. It contains about 600 words. These words may be names of people who appear in the Bible, for example, Elijah, or they may be a subject such as the 'Lord's Supper'. There is also a listing of the miracles and parables of Jesus.

WHAT IS THE BIBLE?

Although one book, the Bible contains sixty-six individual books. Within each of these there is often a variety of writing such as poetry, prose, biography, letters, family trees, official records, songs and prayers. It is important to recognise the type of writing when we are reading so that we read the Bible on its own terms. To read poetry, for example, as if it was an excerpt from an official record, would make it very difficult to understand.

POETRY

The main division is between prose and poetry. Several of the Old Testament books are written completely in poetry: Psalms, the Song of Songs and Lamentations for instance. Most of the book of Job is written in poetic form, and other poems are found in prose passages, for example, Exodus 15; Judges 5 and 1 Samuel 2. Modern translations show quite clearly where poetry is used and it is easy to see that most of the prophetic books are written in poetic form. In the New Testament there is some poetry, for example, Mary's Song (Luke 1:46–55), Zechariah's Song (Luke 1:68–79) and Philippians 2:6–11.

There is an important difference between Hebrew/Jewish poetry and modern poetry. Hebrew poetry uses **rhythm** and not rhyme. It also uses **'parallelism'** which means that the idea or thought in one line is repeated in the next line in a different way and using different words. A glance at any poetic passage will illustrate this, for example:

Job 33:4   'The Spirit of God has made me;
        the breath of the Almighty
        gives me life.'

There are also many **different types of poetry**. The Song of Songs and the book of Job are each written as a play with various actors. In the Psalms there are poetic songs and prayers for many different occasions: songs of thanksgiving, songs for pilgrims, songs for the coronation of a king, prayers for the congregation and prayers for

individuals. In the New Testament it is probable that
Philippians 2:6–11, for example, was a hymn sung by the
first Christians.

*LAW

Israel's laws are found in the books of Exodus through to
Deuteronomy. These formed the foundation of the life of
the nation and of its relationship with God. Thus the law is
regarded as an expression of God's character and will; the
law shows how God wants his people to behave, to worship,
and to live in society.

The best known list of laws is the Ten Commandments
(Exodus 20). These are a summary of the essential points of
the many laws contained in Exodus through to Deuteronomy. Three groups of laws have been drawn out: Covenant Law or the **Book of the *Covenant** (Exodus 21–23),
which contains moral, civil and religious laws. **The Holiness
Code** (Leviticus 17–26) which, as its name suggests, arises
from the frequent statements, 'I the LORD am holy—I
who make you holy' (Leviticus 21:8). This law 'book' sets
out rules for worship, especially about priests and sacrifices. **The Deuteronomic Code** (Deuteronomy 12–25) is
set out like a sermon and includes warnings about the
consequences of breaking the laws.

These laws touch on every area of life, not only religion.
There are laws about family life (marriage etc.), human
rights, theft, damage to property, personal and food
hygiene and so on. Many of them are uncompromising, or
absolute statements: 'You shall/shall not' (as in Exodus
20), but many are what we call 'case laws': 'if . . . then'
—what to do in particular situations.

There are no new lists of commandments in the New
Testament, though some regard the **Sermon on the Mount**
(Matthew 5–7) as the new law for Christians. The standards
set out there are even more difficult to achieve than in the
Old Testament law. Some Christians therefore regard
these as ideals to be aimed at, even if they can never fully
attain them. Paul has much to say about the law (and uses
the word in different ways), but basically he teaches that

while it is good, it is limited. This is because people can never earn God's love—it is given freely.

A SPECIAL KIND OF HISTORY

There is much in the Bible which helps us to piece together the early history of the Jewish nation and later, the early church. The history books of the Old Testament are Joshua through to 2 Kings, and 1 and 2 Chronicles record some of the same events. There are historical passages in Isaiah and Jeremiah, and parts of Genesis, Exodus and Numbers could be described as 'history'. In the New Testament there are some historical references in the Gospels and Acts.

In the Hebrew Bible Joshua–2 Kings are grouped together and called 'The Former Prophets'. This will help us to understand that biblical history is not history told for its own sake, but history told from a particular point of view. It does not tell us everything that happened but only those events which show how God is at work in his world, developing his plan in the Jewish nation and later in the church. This does not mean that this history is unreliable, for archaeology and comparative studies of other nations show it to be trustworthy.

There are many references in the Old Testament books of history which show that the writers and editors used older writings and records. For example Joshua 10:13 and 2 Samuel 1:18 refer to 'The Book of Jashar'; 1 Kings 11:41 to the 'annals of Solomon' and 1 Chronicles 29:29 to 'the records of Nathan the prophet and the records of Gad the seer'. Reference is also made to particular people writing down God's words: Exodus 24:4 (Moses); 1 Samuel 10:25 (Samuel). The many family trees (*genealogies) were other sources used by the writers. In the New Testament the writer of Luke and Acts indicates that he has investigated other accounts (Luke 1:3).

*PROPHECY

There are many prophetic books in the Old Testament and they are grouped together from Isaiah through to Malachi. The popular idea of prophecy is that it is the prediction of future events, but biblical prophecy is much more than this. The prophets announced God's message not only, or necessarily, about the future, but very often about the present. Frequently they began with the words, 'This is what the Lord says'. They spoke God's word and that meant that they condemned social injustice and sham worship. They exposed mistaken, cosy ideas about God and his laws and warned the people that God must punish them if they did not mend their ways.

The prophets communicated what they had to say in many different ways: dialogue, narrative, poetry, picture language and drama. Many prophets have given us an account of how God called them to their work. Their conviction was that they said what God had told them to say, but how they received those words we do not know.

There are a few references to prophets writing down at least some of their message: Isaiah 30:8 (Isaiah), and Jeremiah 30:2 (Jeremiah). Jeremiah 36 also tells us that Jeremiah dictated some of his message to Baruch who must have been a follower of his.

Other prophecies have both an immediate and a long term meaning; they were fulfilled in the prophet's lifetime or soon after, but only partly so. The New Testament writers understood this and show how many of the Old Testament promises were finally fulfilled in the life, death and resurrection of Jesus.

APOCALYPTIC

This is a particular type of prophetic literature found notably in Daniel (chapters 6–12) and Revelation, but also in Isaiah 24–27, Ezekiel 38–39, Zechariah 9–14 (the first part of the book is apocalyptic in thought) and Mark 13, which is known as 'the little Apocalypse'. The word comes from Greek, and means 'unveiling' or 'revealing' and the book of Revelation is often called 'The Apocalypse' since it is the unveiling or revealing of the future. Apocalyptic writing is full of strange symbols and creatures, as well as angels. The interpretation of apocalyptic writing gives rise to a variety of points of view.

WISDOM

We know that many ancient nations had 'wisdom writings'. Job, Ecclesiastes and Proverbs are the main biblical Wisdom books, but many of the Psalms belong to this type of writing (for example, 1, 34, 37, 73 etc). Wisdom writing was interested in the problems of existence: why are we here? why are things the way they are? why do people suffer? In its simplest and earliest form wisdom was communicated in riddles (Judges 14:14; 1 Samuel 24:13 for example) and the proverbs found in the biblical book of that name. The book of Proverbs is full of statements and observations, often amusing, about life. Sometimes they are presented as if a father or teacher were talking to his son or student, teaching him how to behave in various situations.

GOSPEL

Although there are four Gospels the word actually applies to what they contain, for the announcement that a new age has begun with Jesus is the gospel, which means 'good news'. The Gospels are, nevertheless, a new and particular kind of biblical literature. It is important to understand that the Gospels are not biographies; they do not simply recount the life of Jesus. Rather, each Gospel presents the story of Jesus from a particular viewpoint, and each has a distinctive way of telling the story. Matthew has grouped Jesus' teaching together; Mark is a vivid, fast-moving story; Luke has beautiful pen sketches of many of the people who featured in the story of Jesus; John is a deeply religious, almost otherworldly study.

Scholars have discussed the writing of the Gospels a great deal. A very early record tells us that Mark wrote down Peter's memories of Jesus. Luke was probably written by the man who helped Paul on some of his missionary work.

LETTERS

The writers of the New Testament letters follow the 'rules' for letter writing of the first century A.D. This began with an opening sentence giving the name of the writer and the recipient. Then followed a general greeting and enquiry into the health of the recipient. The main section of the letter was concluded with a personal greeting. However, the New Testament letters are much longer than the average 150–200 words of the letters of that period. Even Philemon, the shortest, is 470 words. Paul's letters are usually characterised by a main section which deals first with teaching and then with the way Christians should put into practice what they have learned. Although most of the New Testament letters tell us the name of the author some do not.

There are some interesting letters in the Old Testament. The best example is in Jeremiah 29, but others are found in 1 Kings 21; 2 Chronicles 30; Ezra 4 and 5 and Nehemiah 6.

ARRANGEMENT OF THE BIBLE

The Old Testament is 'The Bible' for both Jews and Christians. In the Christian Bible the New Testament is added. This table shows how the writings are arranged in both the English (Christian) and Jewish Bibles.

ENGLISH		JEWISH
The Pentateuch		*Torah (Law)*
Genesis	=	Bereshith (In the beginning)
Exodus	=	Shemoth (Names)
Leviticus	=	Wayiqra (And he called)
Numbers	=	Bemidbar (In the wilderness)
Deuteronomy	=	Debarim (Words)
The Historical Books		*Nebi'im (Prophets)*
		FORMER PROPHETS
Joshua	=	Yehoshua
Judges	=	Shofetim
Ruth		
1 Samuel		
2 Samuel	= }	Shemuel
1 Kings		
2 Kings	= }	Melakim
1 Chronicles		LATTER PROPHETS
2 Chronicles		Yeshayahu (Isaiah)
Ezra		Yirmeyahu (Jeremiah)
Nehemiah		Yehezqel (Ezekiel)
Esther		Tere Asar (Twelve) Minor Prophets
The Poetic Books		*Kethubim (Writings)*
Job		
Psalms	=	Tehillim (Praises)
Proverbs	=	Mishle (Proverbs of)
Ecclesiastes		Iyyob (Job)
Song of Songs		Shir Hashirmim (Song of Songs) ⎫
		Ruth ⎪ The
		Ekah (= 'How') (Lamentations) ⎬ Five
		Qoheleth (Ecclesiastes) ⎪ Scrolls
		Ester (Esther) ⎭
		Daniel
		Ezra-Nehemiah
		Dibre Hayyamim (Chronicles)

ENGLISH

JEWISH
See LATTER PROPHETS

The Prophetic Books
MAJOR: Isaiah
Jeremiah
Lamentations
Ezekiel
Daniel
MINOR: Hosea
Joel
Amos
Obadiah
Jonah
Micah
Nahum
Habakkuk
Zephaniah
Haggai
Zechariah
Malachi

The New Testament
Gospels
Acts
Letters
Revelation

HOW WE GOT OUR BIBLE

Our modern versions of the Bible are the result of a long process going back hundreds of years, a process involving writers, editors, translators and scholars. Christians consider that the origin and ultimate author of the Bible is God, but it is also clear that he has used human gifts and skills in the process of putting his message into writing. 2 Timothy 3:16 says that 'all Scripture is God-breathed' and 2 Peter 1:21 that 'men spoke from God as they were carried along by the Holy Spirit', a claim that God communicated his words in some way through people. In the same way it is reasonable to imagine that God worked through those who were involved in the process of writing down and translating his message.

HOW THE BIBLE WAS WRITTEN

The Bible is divided into the Old Testament and the New Testament. The word **'testament'** is a translation of a Greek word which means **'covenant'**. The Old Testament is about the old covenant or agreement made between God and Israel and based on the *Law. The New Testament is about the new agreement made between God and his people and based on Jesus' death and resurrection.

THE OLD TESTAMENT: Here is a simple summary of how the Old Testament became what it is.

1. Written accounts, often using older writings, were carefully preserved from the earliest times and verified by oral tradition. These were collected together.

2. Editing and re-editing brought together collections of material and new material was added. Groups of prophets (called 'schools') saved the work of the great prophets. Scholars, known as 'scribes' edited and updated the books, thereby passing on a living tradition. This work was most important during the time in exile, and great care would have been taken to preserve sacred writings.

THE NEW TESTAMENT: In some ways this is a more

clear-cut process. The letters of Paul are probably the earliest writings of the New Testament and they were no doubt preserved in the communities to which they were addressed. By the end of the first century A.D. they were combined in one collection.

The story of Jesus' death and resurrection (the Passion Narrative) probably existed in written form from an early period. The Gospels themselves probably developed in a similar way to the Old Testament: oral and written traditions alongside each other. The Apostles would have had first-hand knowledge of the words of Jesus, but as they began to die the need to write down these words would have been realised.

HOW THE BOOKS OF THE BIBLE WERE SELECTED

The Old Testament is the Hebrew or Jewish Bible, while the Christian Bible includes Old and New Testaments. The list of the books included in the Bible is called **'the canon'**. 'Canon' comes from a Greek word meaning 'rule' or 'measure', and referred originally to the 'reed' used as a ruler. Thus the Old Testament canon is the list of books which the Jews regarded as inspired and therefore the authoritative yardstick for belief and behaviour.

We do not really know how the Old Testament canon was finally agreed. We can only guess that the requirements for including a book (apart from the helpfulness of what was in the book) was that it was connected with a spiritual leader. Thus the Pentateuch is connected with Moses, Psalms with David, Proverbs with Solomon and so on.

We do have clear evidence that by the fifth century B.C. the Pentateuch was fixed and regarded as authoritative, probably as a result of the work of Ezra (the 'Law of Moses' referred to in Nehemiah 8 was almost certainly the Pentateuch).

Work probably continued on the Prophets and Writings and by 165 B.C. these two groups were fixed. By the beginning of the New Testament period the identity of every Old Testament book was accepted, although debate continued over Ezekiel, Proverbs, the Song of Songs, Ecclesiastes and Esther.

The process of deciding which books should belong in the New Testament is uncertain. The collection of Paul's letters was the first stage. By the end of the second century A.D. we know that there were four Gospels (and no others) in use, and that Acts was also accepted. 1 Peter and 1 John must have been recognised soon after this. There was some doubt about James, Hebrews, Revelation, 2 and 3 John, 2 Peter and Jude, but by the third century A.D. a definite list was in existence though debate continued into the fourth century A.D.

ORAL AND WRITTEN TRADITIONS

The books of the Old Testament cover a period of at least a thousand years, and those of the New Testament some sixty years. The written records themselves fall roughly within the period 2000 B.C.–A.D. 100. How did they survive and how were they kept?

In two ways: orally and in writing. **'Oral tradition'** means the passing on of information by word of mouth. In the ancient world (as in certain cultures today) important information, traditions and stories were handed on from generation to generation and from person to person in songs, anecdotes, poetry, proverbs etc. In such cultures people have very accurate memories and oral tradition was an important way of spreading information.

At the same time **writing** existed from at least the third millennium B.C., and possibly even from the fourth. Records were scratched on stone, clay, potsherds (known as 'ostraca'), wood and ivory. Cuneiform script was the earliest form of writing: it was made by impressing a wedge-shaped implement onto wet clay. Thousands of cuneiform inscriptions, including letters, official records, rule books and stories from Egypt and Mesopotamia, and some from Palestine, show us that writing was widely used throughout the ancient world.

Later papyrus (made from the papyrus plant growing along the Nile) was used and made into scrolls. The famous

Dead Sea Scrolls discovered in 1947 included copies of
every Old Testament book except Esther and date from the
first century B.C.

It was probably during the second century A.D. that the
first books appeared. The pages were stitched together and
the 'book' known as a 'codex'.

LANGUAGES

Three languages were used by the first biblical writers:

Hebrew is the main language of the Old Testament, a
language of the 'Semitic' group, spoken throughout
Mesopotamia.

Aramaic was the language of commerce towards the end
of the Old Testament period and was the spoken
language of Palestine at the time of Jesus. A few
passages in Ezra and Daniel, and Jeremiah 10:11, are
Aramaic, and some Aramaic words are used by the
Gospel writers.

Greek. The New Testament was written in Greek, but a
particular type known as 'common Greek'—a sim-
plified form of classical Greek. The Greek language
was used throughout the world of the New Testament. There was a Greek version of the Old Testament known as the **'Septuagint'** (often denoted by the
Roman numerals 'LXX' because the tradition is that
seventy scholars translated it), translated in Alexandria in Egypt in the third century B.C.

TRANSLATING THE BIBLE

The earliest copies of parts of the Hebrew Old Testament
were found at Qumran in 1947. These **'Dead Sea Scrolls'**
date to the first century B.C. Before this discovery our
earliest manuscripts were ninth century A.D., although
these were copies and not originals (scribal copying was
meticulous and since the text was regarded as sacred much
thought was given to its preservation). The discoveries at
Qumran also gave earlier evidence of the Greek text of the
Old Testament. We also have some Greek papyri from the
third and fourth centuries which include fragments of

Deuteronomy, a lot of Numbers, parts of Isaiah, Ezekiel, Daniel and Esther.

During the sixth to the tenth centuries A.D. the Hebrew text was carefully copied by the successors to the earlier scribes, called **the 'Masoretes'**. Their work is preserved in what is called the **'Masoretic text'**—a highly valued tool for translators.

For the New Testament more manuscripts are available. A fragment of John dates from A.D. 130 (John Rylands papyrus), and there are third and fourth century papyri of other scraps of John's Gospel, most of Paul's letters, parts of the Gospels, and Acts. There are hundreds of codices ('books') dating from the fourth to the ninth centuries. The most important are the:

Codex Sinaiticus (complete New Testament dating from the fourth century)

Codex Alexandrinus (most of the New Testament dating from the fifth century)

Codex Vaticanus (dating from the fifth century).

Our twentieth-century Bible is therefore the result of centuries of comparison and study of all the available manuscripts and translations (for which there are comparatively few for the Old Testament and almost too many for the New!) with the aim of establishing the original text.

HOW WE GOT OUR BIBLE

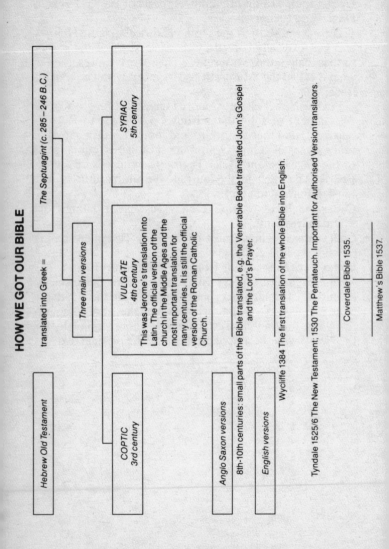

Hebrew Old Testament

The Septuagint (c. 285 – 246 B.C.)

translated into Greek =

Three main versions

COPTIC
3rd century

SYRIAC
5th century

VULGATE
4th century

This was Jerome's translation into Latin. The official version of the church in the Middle Ages and the most important translation for many centuries. It is still the official version of the Roman Catholic Church.

Anglo Saxon versions

8th-10th centuries: small parts of the Bible translated, e.g. the Venerable Bede translated John's Gospel and the Lord's Prayer.

English versions

Wycliffe 1384 The first translation of the whole Bible into English.

Tyndale 1525/6 The New Testament; 1530 The Pentateuch. Important for Authorised Version translators.

Coverdale Bible 1535.

Matthew's Bible 1537.

The Great Bible 1539. Important influence on history of subsequent translation.

Bishop's Bible 1568.

Authorised Version (King James Version) 1611. First translation by a group of scholars rather than an individual.

Revised Version 1881. Used some early manuscripts as well as the earlier English versions.

American Standard Version 1901.

Revised Standard Version 1946. (New Testament); 1952 (Old Testament).

New English Bible 1961 (New Testament); 1970 (Old Testament).

New American Standard Bible 1963 (New Testament); 1970 (Old Testament).

Jerusalem Bible 1966 (New Testament); 1976 (Old Testament).

Good News Bible 1966 (New Testament); 1976 (Old Testament).

New International Version 1973 (New Testament); 1978 (Old Testament).

PLAN OF THE BIBLE

GENESIS

As its name implies this book is about origins or beginnings
—of the universe, of the different nations, of *sin, and of
the Jewish people. The first eleven chapters reach back to
the beginning of time and deal with questions that we all
ask: who made the world? where did we come from? why is
there suffering and evil in the world?

In chapters 12–50 we move from the general (the human
race) to the particular as we learn how God moved into the
chaos and confusion and chose one man, Abraham. God
directed him to settle in the land of Israel and he and his
descendants, Isaac and Jacob, are known as the patriarchs
(fathers) or founders of Israel. Jacob's twelve sons were the
beginnings of the twelve tribes. Through Joseph, one of his
sons, the whole family settled in Egypt.

EXODUS

The centre-piece of this book is God's deliverance of
emergent Israel from Egypt and the book's name means
'going out'. Some four hundred years separate Genesis and
Exodus, during which time Egyptian attitudes to the settlers changed from peaceful co-existence to hostility and
oppression. Moses emerged to lead God's people out of
Egypt, their destination being the land of Israel. At the
mountain of *Sinai God gave Moses the laws which were to
form the basis of the newly-formed nation's life. These are
summed up in the *Ten Commandments.

LEVITICUS

This is a book of further laws or rules, mainly for Israel's
worship, and in particular about *sacrifice and the *priesthood. A key word is *'holiness', for the intention of the laws
was to help the people relate to God and in so doing to
reflect his character in daily life.

NUMBERS

The first ten chapters continue in the legal atmosphere of

Leviticus. The name of the book arises from the various censuses or numberings taken prior to breaking camp and leaving Sinai. The remaining chapters are a sad record of almost forty years wandering in the desert and of complaints and rebellion against Moses and God.

DEUTERONOMY

The setting of the book is the border of the land of Israel. It is presented as three sermons of Moses in which he surveys the journey from Egypt, the people's rebellion and God's patient loyalty. He restates and underlines some of the laws of Exodus, Leviticus and Numbers (thus the book's title, which means 'second law-giving'), and stresses the need for obedience after they have settled in Israel. The book closes with some final words of Moses and his death.

JOSHUA

The first twelve chapters tell us about the initial occupation of Israel under its new leader, Joshua. The remaining chapters outline the planned territorial division among the twelve tribes. Many of the native people still had to be conquered.

JUDGES

This book continues the story of the conquest of the land of Israel which involved conflict with various tribes both in and around Israel. Interwoven in the account is the constant disobedience to God alternating with a turning back to him, and his patient loyalty which is demonstrated in various leaders (called *'judges') who emerged to rally the tribes to fight their enemies.

RUTH

This is a story of family loyalty and loyalty to God and to his laws. It is set in the same period as Judges. The central character, Ruth, was not an Israelite but came to believe in God and, through her marriage to an Israelite called Boaz, became the great-grandmother of David and an ancestor of Jesus.

1 SAMUEL

The first and second books of Samuel recount Israel's history in the crucial transition from intermittent leadership to monarchy. The books take their name from the prophet who appointed the first two kings, Saul and David.

1 Samuel picks up from the book of Judges and shows how the continued harassment from neighbouring tribes made the people ask for a king.

2 SAMUEL

This is about Israel's second, and best known king, David. The book opens against a background of civil war following the death of Saul in battle. Later in the book we read of intrigue among David's sons over the succession. It was David who established Jerusalem as Israel's capital.

1 KINGS

The two books of Kings cover the history of Israel over a period of almost four hundred years.

The first eleven chapters of 1 Kings concern David's son, Solomon, the third king of Israel. His importance centres on his building of the Jerusalem Temple, the focal point of Israel's worship. His son, Rehoboam, inherited a dissatisfied nation and due to his foolish attitude ten of the tribes formed themselves into a separate state under a former official of Solomon's called Jeroboam. Subsequently this state is known as Israel, or the Northern Kingdom, and the remaining two tribes as Judah, or the Southern Kingdom. The history of these two states is recounted in interwoven accounts in the remaining chapters of 1 and 2 Kings. Elijah, an important prophet, dominates the end of 1 Kings.

2 KINGS

The death of Elijah and the emergence of the prophet Elisha occupy the early chapters of 2 Kings. The remaining sweep of the history covers some three hundred years, and from a religious point of view is all downhill apart from one or two religious revivals promoted by the reigning monarch. The end of the Northern Kingdom comes a century and a half before that of Judah, but in both cases it is understood as the inevitable punishment for turning away from God.

1 CHRONICLES

The two books of Chronicles cover the same period as Samuel and Kings but from a particular point of view. The writer, known as 'The Chronicler', shows that David laid the foundations of Israel's worship even though he did not build the Temple. In the first nine chapters he uses family trees to trace the history of Israel from Adam to the return from Exile to show that Judah is the true people of God.

2 CHRONICLES

Solomon, the builder of the Temple, is the subject of chapters 1–9. It becomes obvious in the remaining chapters that interest lies only in the history of Judah, through whom God would continue his purpose. Special attention is also given to kings who promoted religious reform. The end of the book goes beyond 2 Kings as it hints that the period in *exile in Babylon is about to end. Persia has taken over the Babylonian empire.

EZRA

This follows on in time immediately from 2 Chronicles. The Persian king has issued a decree which allows the Jews to return to Israel and to rebuild the Jerusalem Temple. In chapters 3–6 we learn that initially the altar was rebuilt and sacrifices resumed but opposition halted the Temple rebuilding for many years. Finally, it was completed and dedicated. Some time later (chapters 7–10) Ezra, an expert on the Jewish law, was sent from Babylon to help and guide the newly-established community. The main problem was that the Jews were intermarrying with other nations, thereby threatening the survival of national identity.

NEHEMIAH

Another leader in establishing the new community, Nehemiah organised the rebuilding of the walls round

Jerusalem, so vital to its security (chapters 1–7). Once this was done Ezra read the law (from the first five books of the Bible) to the people and led them in a confession of their disobedience to God and then to a promise to obey him in the future (chapters 8–10). Nehemiah also carried through several social reforms (chapters 11–13).

ESTHER

The setting of this story is the Persian king's palace in the same period as Ezra–Nehemiah. Esther, a Jew, became a Persian queen and was able to save the Jews in the Persian empire from a plot to exterminate them.

JOB

The story of Job is found in the first two and the last chapter of the book. *Satan is allowed to bring several major tragedies into the life of this good and religious man. The main section of the book is a discussion between Job and three friends (a fourth makes a brief appearance) as to why Job has suffered so much trouble. The questions raised are not only about human suffering but about God: is he fair? is he even good? Traditional, trite answers are shown to be inadequate.

PSALMS

Here are sacred songs, poems and prayers which originated in Israel's worship and her experience of God. They are traditionally associated with David but reflect centuries of individual and corporate responses to God. Human emotions of anger, despair, sadness, guilt, doubt, joy, praise and adoration are expressed. Themes include the *Law, Jerusalem and its Temple, Israel's history, the natural world, human suffering and God's justice.

PROVERBS

The first nine chapters are written as though a father, or perhaps a teacher, is giving advice to a son or student. After this each verse presents a proverb as we know proverbs today—concise, common sense and often witty statements about wise, successful living. Dominant themes include: poverty, justice, pride, self-control, drunkenness, anger, speaking wisely.

ECCLESIASTES

The name of this book means something like 'The Teacher' and the central word is 'meaningless'. The writer examines every aspect of life: wealth, social position, professional success and pleasure and concludes that they are futile because of the fact of death which comes to everyone. The only positive suggestion is that we should enjoy whatever God has given us, and in chapter 12:13 the Teacher states his conclusion: 'Fear God and keep his Commandments'.

SONG OF SONGS

This is presented in poetic form as a 'song' about the wonder of sexual love. There are at least two individual speakers, a man and a woman, and a group called 'friends'. There are conversations between them, but also thoughts of each lover about the other. Many see the Song as a symbol of God's love for his people.

ISAIAH

This book relates to a period of some three hundred years. Chapters 1–39 are set in the closing years of the Northern Kingdom when Judah was still relatively safe. Isaiah worked in Jerusalem warning its people that God's judgment must fall on them because of social injustice and religious hypocrisy. To successive kings of Judah he advised dependence on God's guidance and protection rather than on political alliances with foreign nations. Jerusalem is spared the same fate as the Northern Kingdom for the time being.

Chapters 40–55 are concerned with the Jewish exiles in Babylon. The message is one of comfort: God is about to do something new and the punishment and pain of the past are over. The return to the land of Israel will recall the deliverance from Egypt.

In the final section of the book, which is set in the period

after the Temple had been rebuilt, there is evidence that
the new community is in danger of slipping back into old
patterns of behaviour. Alongside warnings is a vision of the
greatness of God and his plans for the blessing of the Jews,
and through them, of all nations.

JEREMIAH

This prophet worked in the closing years of Judah. His
message was one of warning: God's judgment must come if
the people persist in rebelling against him. Indeed, judgment has become inevitable and they would be wise to
recognise that God was using Babylon to punish them.
When the ruling classes were exiled to Babylon Jeremiah
told them that God would work out his plans through the
exiles. At the same time he tried to encourage those who
remained in Judah to accept their fate, but his words fell on
deaf ears. Within the book we have several insights into
what this unpopular prophet was thinking and feeling.

LAMENTATIONS

This is a funeral song about the devastated city of Jerusalem, possibly written by Jeremiah. Each chapter is a
complete poem and in each the mood changes from anguish
and despair in the recognition that punishment was de-
served, to hope in God's love and mercy. Prayer is made
that God will once again show these to his people.

EZEKIEL

This prophet was exiled to Babylon and his work was
among the exiles there. He may have been a priest and a
key theme of the book is God's *holiness. The book is full
of strange symbolism, visions and accounts of how the
prophet often presented his message through drama.
Roughly, the first thirty-three chapters convey a similar
message to that of Jeremiah and at a similar period: Jerusalem will be captured by Babylon and the Temple will be
destroyed. Once this had taken place Ezekiel's message
was one of comfort (chapters 33–39): God will bring back
his people to their own country one day. Meanwhile, in

Babylon they will learn that God can be worshipped even though there is no temple or they cannot offer *sacrifice. Chapters 40–48 are a detailed vision of the future which centres on the Temple.

DANIEL

Daniel was also an exile in Babylon but was chosen to live in the Babylonian court and to train for the civil service. Despite this privilege we learn that Daniel, and later three of his friends, refused to give up their Jewish faith. God blessed their loyalty and Daniel was respected and con-sulted by the Babylonian, and later the Persian kings, particularly because of his ability to interpret dreams. The second part of the book (chapters 7–12) includes some detailed visions full of strange symbols and not always easy to interpret.

HOSEA

This prophet lived and worked in the Northern Kingdom in the closing years of its existence. Through his own experi-ence of a broken marriage Hosea gained a deep insight into Israel's relationship to God. The *covenant made at Sinai was like a marriage, but like Hosea's own wife Israel had left God to worship Canaanite gods. Hosea speaks mov-ingly of the sadness God feels because of his love for Israel even though she deserves to be punished.

JOEL

We are not sure when Joel lived. In chapter 1 he speaks of the devastation caused by a plague of locusts. This may have been a real event or a vision but in either case it is a symbol of the invading army which God will use to punish his people (2:1–11). Joel calls the people to turn back to God while there is still time and speaks of a special out-pouring of God's Spirit (2:12–32). Chapter 3 concerns a final and universal judgment.

AMOS

This prophet came from the Southern Kingdom but worked

in the Northern Kingdom slightly earlier than Hosea. In chapters 1–2 he speaks of God's judgment on the surrounding nations but also on the complacent Northern Kingdom. In chapter 3 he announces that God has broken off the *covenant agreement with his people in the Northern Kingdom and the next few chapters show why: oppression, social injustice, religious hypocrisy. Five visions (chapters 7–9) show that there is still time to turn back to God, but in the last two visions punishment is inevitable. A hope for something beyond God's judgment is expressed in the last few verses.

OBADIAH

This is the shortest Old Testament book and we know nothing about the prophet. The theme is the punishment of Edom, which lay to the south-east of the Dead Sea. The Edomites were descendants of Esau and thus related to the Israelites, yet they were longstanding enemies. The reference in this book suggests that when Jerusalem fell to the Babylonian army in 587 B.C. the Edomites did nothing to help and maybe even took some advantage of Judah's fate. While Edom disappeared from history Obadiah foretells the return of Israel to her own land.

JONAH

God told the prophet Jonah to go and warn the people of Nineveh, capital of Assyria (a cruel enemy of Israel) that God was going to punish her. After attempts to evade God's orders Jonah reluctantly preached in the city and the Ninevites turned to God. Jonah was furious with God for showing mercy to such wicked people and God tries to demonstrate to the prophet that he feels compassion even for Israel's enemies.

MICAH

This prophet lived and worked a little later than Amos and Hosea and about the same time as Isaiah and what he has to say is very similar to them. He worked in the Southern Kingdom and condemned social injustice and inequality, and corruption among the political and religious leaders. God must punish his people but beyond that Micah speaks of a future which will centre on the Jerusalem Temple when a descendant of David will emerge to lead God's people against her enemies (chapters 4–7). Chapter 6:6–8 seems to sum up the message, not only of Micah, but of all the prophets of this period.

NAHUM

This prophet announces the destruction of Nineveh, capital of Assyria. In the opening verses Nahum speaks of God as 'slow to anger' but also that he will 'not leave the guilty unpunished'. It is for this reason that God must now punish Nineveh for extreme cruelty. Chapters 2 and 3 are a poem about the siege of Nineveh. This took place in 612 B.C.

HABAKKUK

Because Habakkuk mentions Babylon (1:6) it is assumed that he worked at the end of the seventh century B.C. The prophet questions God about his justice: why does he turn a blind eye to cruelty and wickedness? How can he use wicked people to punish people who are better than them? God gives no direct answer (chapter 2) but promises that one day he will punish all oppression and injustice. Chapter 3 is a poem about God coming to punish all wickedness and concludes with a statement by the prophet of his trust in God, no matter what happens.

ZEPHANIAH

Zephaniah worked just before Jeremiah. The theme of the book is God's universal judgment. Chapter 1 deals with the judgment of Israel but chapter 2:1–3 promises that this may be averted if they turn back to God. The remainder of chapter 2 foretells the punishment of some of Israel's neighbours. Beyond the judgment of Jerusalem the prophet sees hope (chapter 3).

HAGGAI

Haggai and Zechariah belong to the same period (520 B.C.).

Many Jews had returned to Israel to rebuild their national life. Initially they worked with enthusiasm but opposition brought the work of rebuilding the Temple to a standstill. Haggai rallied the people, showing that the economic difficulties they were experiencing were because they had their priorities wrong. The important thing for their national life was God's 'house' and God had greater things in store if they would only learn to put him first.

ZECHARIAH

Like Haggai, this prophet encouraged the people to take up the work they had left off and complete the Temple building. His messages are given in a series of visions in chapters 1–8 and concern other issues as well as the rebuilding. Chapters 9–14 are in a different form, more typical of prophetic messages. Their theme is the future age: Israel's deliverance, God's triumph and the work of the Messiah.

MALACHI

This book indicates that after the time of Haggai and Zechariah things deteriorated again. The people felt disappointed with God (1:2–5), the religious leaders were corrupt and slipshod in their duties (1:6–2:9), and everybody disobedient to God's laws (2:10–16) while at the same time treating him with contempt (2:17–3:18). Chapter 4 looks forward to the time when injustice will be dealt with and those who are loyal to God will be restored.

MATTHEW

The first three Gospels follow a similar pattern and are often known as the 'Synoptic Gospels' because they 'see together' the life of Jesus. Yet each has its own particular emphasis.

Matthew begins by tracing Jesus' family history back to Abraham and recounts various incidents concerned with Jesus' birth (chapters 1–2). His is a carefully organised Gospel and he is especially interested in what Jesus said: the Sermon on the Mount (chapters 5–7), *parables about the *kingdom of heaven (chapter 13) and parables about the end of time (chapter 25). He also shows that Jesus is the Messiah spoken of in the Old Testament.

MARK

This Gospel concentrates mainly on what Jesus did, although the writer does include some of Jesus' teaching. Within the first few chapters several miracles are recorded. He does not speak about Jesus' birth but begins with John the Baptist's work and Jesus' baptism and temptations. Chapters 1–9 are about Jesus' work in Galilee, chapters 10–15 his journey to Jerusalem ending in his death, and chapter 16 about his resurrection. Chapter 16:9–20 was added later, probably by the early church.

LUKE

The first two chapters of this Gospel contain several unique incidents related to Jesus' birth and early life. Luke traces Jesus' family tree to Adam, which underlines the emphasis on Jesus as the Saviour of the whole world. He stresses that Jesus is concerned for minority groups, for the poor and the oppressed. Other prominent themes are prayer, joy and the *Holy Spirit. He often cross-references events to dates in secular history. He is also the author of Acts.

JOHN

It is obvious from the first verse that this Gospel is very different in atmosphere to the other three. Jesus' miracles are called 'signs', Jesus does not speak of the *'kingdom' but of 'eternal life'. There are no parables but several long, rather complex sermons which are usually linked to one of the signs. Thus when Jesus heals a blind man he speaks of himself as 'the light of the world'. These 'I am' sayings are quite distinctive to this Gospel and the accounts of Jesus' appearances after his resurrection are also unique.

ACTS

This is the 'second instalment' of the story begun in Luke's Gospel and tells us what happened in the early church in the first thirty years or so. It begins with the ascension of Jesus (chapter 1) and the coming of the Holy Spirit at Pentecost (chapter 2). The next ten chapters show how the gospel spread beyond the locality of Jerusalem as far as Samaria. Peter, Stephen and James are the main characters. Chapters 13–28 centre on Paul and his three missionary tours taking the gospel to Greece and Europe. The whole book shows that the main source of opposition to the 'new religion' came from the Jews, not the Roman government.

ROMANS

This is the first of twenty-one letters found in the New Testament. They are very important because they give us an inside view of life in the earliest Christian churches and the teaching of their leaders. Paul had not been to Rome when he wrote this letter. It is the most detailed account of an important part of his teaching: that the only way to be accepted by God is to rely on what Jesus did through his death and resurrection (chapters 1–8). In chapters 9–11 Paul expresses the hope that although the Jews have largely refused this teaching they will one day accept it. Romans follows the pattern of most of Paul's letters: the first part is teaching and the second practical application in real life. Thus chapters 12–16 speak of how Christians should behave in the Church and in the world.

1 CORINTHIANS

This and the following letter were written to a church in the Greek city of Corinth which Paul had visited (Acts 18: 1–21). Paul had heard that there were various problems in the church: party politics (chapters 1–4), moral problems (chapter 5), Christians taking each other to court (chapter 6), marriage (chapter 7), special difficulties arising from living in a city full of temples to various gods (chapters 8–10), the organisation of worship (chapters 11–14) and intellectual problems with life after death (chapter 15).

2 CORINTHIANS

Between this and the previous letter Paul visited the church. There had been a lot of criticism and even hostility

shown to him, and his authority as a leader had been called
into question. Relationships had improved but Paul found
it necessary to stress the genuineness of his authority as
an *apostle (chapters 2–3, 10–13). The letter shows how
deeply Paul felt (chapter 7). Chapter 5 contains further
teaching on life after death, and chapters 8–9 give details
about an appeal for financial help for a group of churches
facing hardship.

GALATIANS

This is probably the first of Paul's letters and its theme is
similar to that of Romans. It is apparent that many Jews felt
that non-Jews becoming Christians should keep the Jewish
law and in particular the food laws, and be *circumcised.
(Acts also tells us this.) The heart of Paul's teaching on this
view is found in 2:14–21: a right relationship with God is
possible only through Jesus, and nothing else is required.
Chapters 5–6 show that this does not mean we can do as we
like. Christians are called to 'serve one another in love' and
the Holy Spirit is given to help them do this.

EPHESIANS

This letter may have been written to several churches in and
around the important city of Ephesus. Paul founded this
church on his third missionary tour (Acts 18:23–20:1). The
clear theme of the letter is unity: God's plan is to bring to an
end all that divides men and women, social classes, cultures, nations and religions. Jesus Christ is the unifying
force, as the head 'unites' the human body. Chapters 4–6
show that this unity is very practical: it is worked out in
good relationships in the family, the church and the work
place.

PHILIPPIANS

Paul established this church on his second missionary tour
(Acts 16:6–40), and this letter was written some ten or
twelve years after that visit. It is a warm, personal letter to a
church for which he felt a deep affection. He speaks of his
imprisonment which has resulted in the gospel being

preached to Roman personnel (chapter 1). Chapter 2
contains an important statement about Jesus as the servant
who was willing to give up his rights for the good of others,
and Paul encourages the church to follow that example.

COLOSSIANS

The church was founded by Epaphras, one of Paul's converts. The contents of the letter make it clear that wrong
teaching was creeping into the church. In the face of this
Paul stresses the true gospel: Jesus is absolutely central. He
existed before time began and he is the one who brings God
and the human race together again (chapter 1). Rituals,
regulations, philosophical reasonings and self-denial are
not what is required (chapter 2) but right relationships and
attitudes in the church, the family, the work place and the
world (chapters 3–4).

1 THESSALONIANS

Paul founded this church on his second missionary tour
(Acts 17:1–9) amid a lot of opposition from Jews. This and
2 Thessalonians are among Paul's earliest letters. No doubt
because the Jews had continued to undermine his reputation Paul begins by insisting that he is a true *apostle
(chapters 1–2). From chapter 3 we learn that Timothy had
been sent to the church and had returned to Paul with an
encouraging report. In chapters 4 and 5 Paul deals with two
questions: what happens to Christians when they die? and
when will Jesus return?

2 THESSALONIANS

The Thessalonian church did not fully understand what
Paul had said in his first letter (1 Thessalonians) about
Jesus' return. They had also been confused by other
teachers who said that Jesus had already returned. Further-
more, some church members had even opted out of re-
sponsibilities on the basis that if Jesus was about to return
there was not much point in going to work! Paul deals with
all these difficulties.

1 TIMOTHY

Paul had met Timothy on his second missionary tour (Acts 16:1–3) and Timothy had worked with him. Now he was a leader in the church at Ephesus and Paul writes to encourage him and give him advice about organising the church there. He writes about public prayer, the appointment of leaders, help for widows and attitudes to slaves (chapters 2–5). He warns about those who teach differently to what has been taught by recognised leaders.

2 TIMOTHY

This is more personal than 1 Timothy and was written at the end of Paul's life. He warns Timothy that wrong teaching is on the increase and people will easily be deceived. In the face of this Timothy must stand by the truth, which will take courage.

TITUS

In a similar way to Timothy, Titus was a leader in the church on the island of Crete. Paul writes as he did in 1 Timothy, about the organisation and leadership of the church, correct teaching in the face of error and right attitudes in the church, the work place and the world.

PHILEMON

Philemon was probably a convert of Paul's and now a church worker. Onesimus, one of his slaves, had run away but had met Paul and become a Christian. Paul writes to Philemon to say that he is sending Onesimus back to his master and appeals to Philemon to do what would have been unusual in those days—to forgive and reinstate Onesimus.

HEBREWS

We do not know who wrote this letter, nor who the readers were. Since the writer's theme is that the Temple and its ceremonies were temporary pointers to Christianity it is probable that the original readers were Jews. The key word for this letter is 'better'. Jesus has offered a better (and the

last) sacrifice (chapters 4–7). He is 'better' than all that has
gone before: greater than the angels (chapters 1–2),
greater than Moses (chapter 3). The New *Covenant has
replaced the Old (chapters 8–10). In the closing chapters he
writes to encourage his readers to keep going in the face of
difficulties and hostility. The people of the Old Testament
did wonderful things because they relied on God (chapter
11). Christians must follow their example and the example
of Jesus (chapter 12).

JAMES

James may have been Jesus' brother who was also the first
leader of the church in Jerusalem. It could be the first of the
New Testament letters to be written, and it is very practical.
The main themes are: if we say we are Christians we must
also live like Christians; discrimination of any kind is
wrong, as is oppression of the poor and the weak; Christians should be self-controlled, especially in what they say.

1 PETER

This letter was written to Christians in the Black Sea coastal
area, probably in the early 60s A.D. The theme is suffering,
and probably the readers were facing real persecution
because they were Christians. Christians must not be sur-
prised if they experience opposition and persecution;
Jesus, their example, certainly did! Indeed, they may be
full of hope and joy because they are sharing with Jesus in
this way. Throughout the letter there are also practical
guidelines on Christian behaviour.

2 PETER

The letter opens with the same emphasis as in 1 Peter on
Christian behaviour. Chapters 2 and 3 are a strong on-
slaught against those who mislead by wrong teaching and
the writer speaks in detail of their future punishment. This
leads him to speak of the return of Jesus.

1 JOHN

It is probable that the writer of this letter and 2 and 3 John

was also the writer of the Gospel of John and the book of
Revelation. It is clear that the Christians to whom he wrote
1 John were worried by teachers of strange ideas. They
were saying they had special understanding of spiritual
matters. This meant that they were claiming to be perfect
on the one hand, and that Jesus could not have been a real
man on the other. In reply John stresses the certainty that
Christians have: 'we know' is a favourite phrase. One of the
clear proofs that people are Christians is that they love
other Christians.

2 JOHN

This letter is written to 'the chosen lady' which probably
refers to a church, not an individual. Some of the themes
found in 1 John are taken up here: loving God means doing
what he has told us to do and loving others. The writer
warns about teachers of wrong ideas.

3 JOHN

This letter is addressed to someone called Gaius who is
praised for the way he is standing by the truth. A man called
Diotrephes is setting himself up as a leader and turning
away representatives of the writer.

JUDE

Many believe that Jude was a brother of Jesus. His letter
uses almost the same words as 2 Peter 2:1–3:3 to condemn
all who mislead by their wrong teaching. He too writes of
their future punishment and encourages his readers to keep
to the teaching they were given originally.

REVELATION

This letter was written to seven churches in Asia Minor
which are named in the course of messages to them from
Jesus in chapters 2–3. John had a vision of Jesus which he
describes in chapter 1. In chapters 4–5 he has another
vision of Jesus and in the course of this Jesus takes a scroll
from the hand 'of him who sat on the throne'. The rest of
the book recounts what happens as Jesus opens this scroll.

These chapters are full of difficult symbols which we do not fully understand and we cannot be certain of their meaning. But the basic message of the book is that God is in control and all evil will eventually be destroyed.

THE BIBLE AT A GLANCE

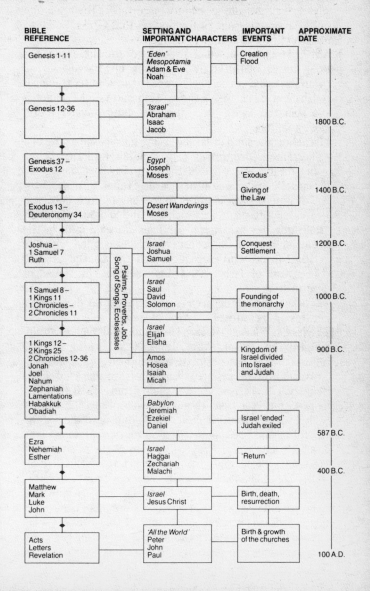

BIBLE REFERENCE	SETTING AND IMPORTANT CHARACTERS	IMPORTANT EVENTS	APPROXIMATE DATE
Genesis 1-11	'Eden' Mesopotamia Adam & Eve Noah	Creation Flood	
Genesis 12-36	'Israel' Abraham Isaac Jacob		1800 B.C.
Genesis 37 – Exodus 12	Egypt Joseph Moses	'Exodus' Giving of the Law	1400 B.C.
Exodus 13 – Deuteronomy 34	Desert Wanderings Moses		
Joshua – 1 Samuel 7 Ruth	Israel Joshua Samuel	Conquest Settlement	1200 B.C.
1 Samuel 8 – 1 Kings 11 1 Chronicles – 2 Chronicles 11	Israel Saul David Solomon	Founding of the monarchy	1000 B.C.
1 Kings 12 – 2 Kings 25 2 Chronicles 12-36 Jonah Joel Nahum Zephaniah Lamentations Habakkuk Obadiah	Israel Elijah Elisha Amos Hosea Isaiah Micah Babylon Jeremiah Ezekiel Daniel	Kingdom of Israel divided into Israel and Judah Israel 'ended' Judah exiled	900 B.C. 587 B.C.
Ezra Nehemiah Esther	Israel Haggai Zechariah Malachi	'Return'	400 B.C.
Matthew Mark Luke John	Israel Jesus Christ	Birth, death, resurrection	
Acts Letters Revelation	'All the World' Peter John Paul	Birth & growth of the churches	100 A.D.

Psalms, Proverbs, Job, Song of Songs, Ecclesiastes

THE LAND AND PEOPLE OF THE BIBLE

GEOGRAPHY

NAME: The place in which the story of the Bible is set has been known by different names in its history:

*   ***Canaan*** is the earliest reference to the country (Genesis 10:19; 11:31). As Genesis 12:6 shows, the name is associated with the people who lived there: Canaanites.

*   ***Israel*** or 'the land of Israel', is the name used as the Old Testament progresses (e.g. 1 Samuel 13:19). When the nation was divided the northern part was called **'Israel'**, and the southern area **'Judah'**. In the New Testament period under the Romans, the land was divided into provinces such as *'Judea' and *'Galilee'.

*   ***Palestine*** has also been used, as for example, in the earlier part of this century. It is associated with the **'Philistines'** who once occupied the coastal area to the west of Israel—the 'land of the Philistines' or 'Philistia'.

    Today, the whole area is so divided that the various titles only confuse!

PHYSICAL FEATURES: The land of Israel is small, roughly the size of Wales, 150–200 miles long and 100 miles at its widest point. It is a land of great contrasts. Travelling in an easterly direction from the Mediterranean Sea there is a coastal plain from which the land slopes gently at first, then more steeply to the central highlands of Judea. It then drops sharply to the Jordan rift valley and rises again to a mountainous plateau in the Trans-Jordan area. Travelling from north to south the land descends steadily from Mount Hermon (9,000 feet) to the Dead Sea (1,275 feet below sea level).

LANDSCAPE: The present landscape is very different from what it was in the early Old Testament period. Then the northern central area and Trans-Jordan were covered by lush forest, and the plains nearer the coast were sand dunes, lagoons, swamp and forest. In the north-west and central areas (where most of the Bible story is set) there were fertile plains. The southern area was desert scrub.

CLIMATE: There are great variations in the climate which falls roughly between temperate and tropical, with wet winters and hot, dry summers (May/June–September/October). Climate varies with the height above sea level, distance from the coast, etc. **Rainfall** is vital and while the rainy season is predictable there are great variations from year to year. In the Bible there are references to:

'the early rains'–mid-October: (Autumn) which make ploughing possible. This is followed by the rainy season proper, November–March, with most *rain falling in December and January.

'the latter rains' or 'spring rains'—vital to mature the grain.

Rainfall averages lessen from north to south and from west to east. During the summer, dew and morning mist bring moisture to the coastal areas and the plains, and this is of vital importance. Drought and famine were constant factors which had to be reckoned with.

OCCUPATIONS:

Agriculture. The people of the Bible, and particularly of Old Testament times, were farmers. Almost everyone would have had their own smallholding, growing what was needed for food, and keeping sheep, goats and cattle. Goats provided milk, and their skins were used to make tents. Sheep provided milk and wool, and occasionally meat. By New Testament times it was fairly common to keep chickens.

Though a large part of the land was desert and rock, and therefore unsuitable for farming, the areas of lower Galilee were fertile. Barley was grown in the fertile valleys (such as the Jordan valley), and wheat in the Plain of Jezreel. Flax for making linen, and millet were also grown. Pomegranates, melons, dates, cucumbers, figs and nuts were important crops providing a supplement to water in the long hot season. On the lower hills there were vineyards—the *vine is an important symbol in the

Bible (e.g. Isaiah 5:7; John 15:1). Olives were eaten for food, and their oil was used for lighting, cooking, medicine, and soap for washing. **Harvesting** began in March (flax) and proceeded with barley (April/May), wheat (May/June), grapes (July–October), figs (August/September) and olives (October/November).

Other Occupations

FISHING: Whole communities made their living from fishing, as the New Testament Gospels show. Lake *Galilee was the focus for this.

MINING: The mining of iron and copper in the area of Ezion Geber began around 1000 B.C. Chemical salts and pitch were found in the Dead Sea area.

POTTERY: Although there are several references to potters and their craft in the Bible, there was nothing distinctive about Israelite pottery.

FROM TENTS TO TOWNS

THE TRIBE: The story of Israel begins with *Abraham. He lived a 'semi-nomadic' life (i.e. travelling from place to place and living in tents) much as the modern Bedouin today. The tribe would include the entire family, from the head of the family/tribe, through the various generations to the youngest member. Servants and large numbers of animals would be included.

EARLY COMMUNITIES: After the settlement in Canaan under Joshua's leadership, the twelve tribes gradually settled into small farming communities or villages, which later became walled towns and cities. Towns were small with about 150–200 houses.

LATER DEVELOPMENTS: Under the kings, and especially Solomon, towns became larger and the gap between rich and poor widened as farms were taken over, and even tenant farmers were forced off their land.

NEW TESTAMENT TIMES: By New Testament times towns were planned more carefully, though life was still quite rural. Jerusalem probably had a quarter of a million inhabitants in the time of Jesus. The Romans, famed for their civil engineering, did much to improve conditions by building drainage schemes, aqueducts etc. They also created 'provinces', some of which were governed by a governor or proconsul, and others (where troops were stationed) by a procurator. Some cities were given special status as Roman colonies and were governed by magistrates. Philippi was one of these. Roman citizenship was another privilege and Paul was proud of his.

HOW PEOPLE LIVED

The Bible covers a period of some 2,000 years so there were changes in some customs and in the way people lived. It is only possible to look at a few of these customs in this section.

FAMILY LIFE:

*Circumcision.** Eight days after birth a boy was circumcised. Other races practised circumcision but it had religious meaning for the Jews. It reminded them that God had chosen them and that they were different from other people.

Education. Learning was based on 'the *Scriptures', particularly the *Laws in the Pentateuch. The many festivals helped children to learn about the history of Israel. Children were taught at home, although by New Testament times boys would go to the *synagogue school. The eldest son succeeded his father. While both boys and girls would help on the farm, girls would also help in the home. Women did all the food preparation, water carrying, spinning, weaving, and the making of clothes.

Marriage. This was arranged by parents, and throughout biblical times there was an insistence that marriage should take place only between fellow Israelites, though many disregarded this, as the Old Testament shows. The **engagement** was binding and a 'bride price' (mohar) would be paid to the bride's father, and a dowry by the bride's father. These could be paid in servants, land, property or work, not only in money. *Divorce** was allowed, but the actual grounds for this were not clear and were still being debated in Jesus' time.

*Death.** There were clear mourning rites which lasted

seven days. The body had to be buried within 24 hours, either in a cave, or for the rich, a specially prepared tomb. There was no clear understanding of a **life beyond death** in the Old Testament. It was believed that the dead went to a 'place of shadows' called 'Sheol'. By the New Testament period the *Pharisees believed in a physical resurrection, and certainly many of the ordinary people did as well (see John 11).

JUSTICE AND ADMINISTRATION:

Early period. After the settlement, when towns began to be established, the entrance ('the gate') became the meeting place and a kind of law-court, where cases were heard and judgment given. Under Solomon an organised administration and government began to emerge, and community and military service was introduced.

Later period. Towards the end of the Old Testament period families of priests began to emerge with wide powers and influence. Together with *'elders' these priests formed a central governing body called **'the *Sanhedrin'** or 'the Council'. It had wide civil and administrative powers and its own police force. It was this court that tried Jesus, and later, some of his followers.

ISRAEL AND HER NEIGHBOURS

Although Israel was a tiny country, its position in relation to the nations which surrounded it gave it a strategic importance. This is because it formed a kind of land bridge between powerful nations: Egypt in the south and Mesopotamia in the north were constantly struggling with each other for possession, influence and control of vital trade routes. An understanding of this helps us to see why, in the Old Testament in particular, there was constant warfare and threat of invasion.

SUMERIA. This probably forms the background culture to Genesis 1–11. It is the oldest culture of which we know, and dates to at least 4500 B.C., so that Sumeria is often called 'the cradle of civilisation'. It lay near the Persian Gulf, between the Tigris and *Euphrates rivers (modern Southern Iraq). Its largest city was **Ur** from which Abraham's family came. Sumerians were scientists, mathematicians and astronomers, but their greatest contribution to civilisation was **writing**, which they seem to have invented. The earliest understandable writing dates from 3200 B.C., and many later languages developed from this. Sumeria had been finally absorbed by the Semites by 1750 B.C., but its legacy of writings lived on.

EGYPT. In Genesis and Exodus the founding fathers of Israel (Abraham, Isaac etc.) travelled constantly to and from Egypt. Egyptian civilisation is very old and reaches back at least to 3000 B.C. It was an advanced culture and Egyptians had special interest in dreams and their interpretation, as well as in poetry, proverbs and story-writing. Their king was called *'Pharaoh' (his Majesty) and was regarded as a god.

At the end of the Old Testament period Egypt's power had dwindled so that she often tried to form political alliances with other nations, including Israel, to keep herself going.

CANAANITES. These were the main racial group in Palestine at the time of the Conquest. They lived in small 'city-states' or 'fortress towns', built on hill summits. Other tribal groups lived alongside them, such as Amorites, Perizzites, etc. (see Exodus 33:2). The significance of the Canaanites for Israel's history is in their religion. This was a nature religion, its chief god being Baal, the storm god, and provider (or withholder) of rain.

*PHILISTINES. They appear to have been part of a general movement of tribes known as 'Sea People', who came to the coastal areas of Palestine from Crete, Cyprus and the Aegean Islands. The territory was known as 'the land of the Philistines' or 'Philistia'. They had five settlements or 'city-states': Gaza, Ashkelon, Gath, Ashdod and Ekron which formed a closely knit and very efficient social and military unit. Their chief god was Dagon.

There was constant border warfare between Israel and the Philistines throughout the period of the Judges and until King David finally defeated them.

SYRIA. Also called *Aram (after the *Aramean tribes who settled here), Syria lay to the north of Israel. Its chief city was *Damascus. Aramaic was probably the language of these early settlers. Relationships between Israel and Syria varied between border warfare, independent existence and alliance.

In the New Testament *Antioch in Syria was an important centre of early Christianity, and it was there that the followers of Jesus were first called Christians.

*ASSYRIA. This lay in north Mesopotamia (the northern part of modern Iraq). It was an ancient nation, settled at least by c. 2300 B.C., but its importance for the history of Israel spans a period of some 200 years (850–650 B.C.) during which Israel became part of the Assyrian empire. Their capital city was Asshur (their chief god had the same name), but later *Nineveh became the capital city until Assyria fell to the Babylonians in 612 B.C. Assyria was a cruel, but very efficient, military nation who resettled conquered peoples away from their own land, thus breaking their national identity. This fate befell the Northern Kingdom of Israel in 722 B.C. Kings mentioned in the Old Testament are **Tiglath-Pileser III** 744–727 B.C. (2 Ki 15:29), **Shalmaneser V** 726–722 B.C. (2 Ki 17:3), **Sargon II** 721–705 B.C. (Isa 20:1), **Sennacherib** 704–681 B.C. (2 Ki 18:13), **Esarhaddon** 681–669 B.C. (2 Ki 19:37) and **Ashurbanipal** 660–627 B.C. (Ezr 4:10).

BABYLON. Babylonian history reaches back to the Sumerian period from which it derives many of its cultural traditions. It lay in what is now Southern Iraq. The Assyrian Empire passed to Babylon under King Nebuchadnezzar. Both *Ezekiel and *Daniel were exiled to Babylon, and Ezra the scribe returned to Israel from Babylon, although by then Babylon had itself fallen to the Persian king, *Cyrus, in 539 B.C.

PERSIA. Persians were originally travelling Indo-Europeans from Southern Russia, who settled in what is now modern Iran about 1000 B.C. Their capital was Susa, where *Nehemiah was based, while the book of *Esther gives an inside view of life in the royal palace there. We

learn about Persian policy towards conquered peoples
from 2 Chronicles and Ezra, both of which contain a
decree of King Cyrus. It shows that Persia encouraged
subject nations to continue their own religion and culture. Kings mentioned in the Old Testament are **Cyrus II**,
the Great (or Darius the Mede) 559–530 B.C. (2 Ch
36:22–23; Ezr 1:1–4; Da 1:21); **Darius I**, the Great
522–486 B.C. (Ezr 4:5; Ne 12:22; Hag 1:1; Zec 1:1),
Artaxerxes 465–424 B.C. (Ezr 7:1, 21–26; Ne 2:1–8),
Darius II 424–404 B.C. (Ne 12:22).

Persian power was overthrown by Alexander the
Great of Greece in 331 B.C.

GREECE. It was Alexander the Great who was responsible for the spread of Greek civilisation throughout the
vast Greek empire. Greek cities were established all over
the empire, and Greek philosophy, science, morality,
customs and language spread everywhere (including
Israel) even after Alexander's death when his empire was
divided between his four generals.

ROME. In 63 B.C. much of Israel was incorporated into the
Roman province of Syria when Pompey marched into
Jerusalem. Over the next few decades there was a lot of
rivalry among Roman leaders, but in 31 B.C. Octavian
emerged as sole ruler of the Empire. In 27 B.C. he took
the name *Augustus and it was during his rule that Jesus
was born (Luke 2:1). Rome brought many benefits to the
world: for example, roads which made travelling and
trade so much easier. Latin and Greek were the official
languages throughout the Empire and this helped the
early Christian missionaries as they went everywhere
preaching.

Despite the fact that subject nations were allowed to
follow their own customs and religion, the Jews hated
Rome. In the time of Jesus Roman troops were stationed
in Judea, and Jewish hopes that God would intervene
and deliver them became very strong. Resistance to
Roman rule increased during the period A.D. 60–70 and
in A.D. 70. Rome retaliated by destroying the Temple in
Jerusalem.

Persecution of Christians seems to have been unusual, but the book of Revelation may indicate a firmer line being taken against the Christian Church.

THE RELIGION OF THE JEWS

THE *LAW

The religion of the Jews is based on their Law, that is to say, the many detailed laws which we find in the Pentateuch, and in particular, Exodus to Deuteronomy. In an earlier section, 'What is the Bible', we looked at the subject of 'Law' and it would be helpful to read that. We saw there that the laws found in the Bible cover agriculture, business, family life, social and moral issues, as well as religion. At the heart of God's Law was his longing for a loving relationship with his people, and all the laws were intended to help them to enjoy that relationship.

*FOOD LAWS. Although these laws are no more important than other groups of laws in the Pentateuch, they did become very significant to the Jews. These laws were rules about which animals, birds and fish could be eaten, how they were to be killed for food, and how they were to be cooked. In the last two centuries before the birth of Jesus (known as 'the Maccabean period') they became an important test of loyalty to the Jewish religion. In the early days of the Christian Church some Christians felt that non-Jewish converts should keep the Jewish food laws.

WORSHIP AND RITUAL

*SACRIFICE. The earliest religious ritual in almost all religions is sacrifice. The first sacrifice in the Bible is that of *Cain and *Abel (Genesis 4), and both *Noah and *Abraham offered sacrifices (and built altars).

In the Law there are detailed instructions about different types of sacrifice, how they were to be offered and what was their purpose. There were animal and bird sacrifices, and offerings of grain cakes, etc. Some sacrifices expressed thanks, some were intended to ask for forgiveness for wrong-doing, some were called 'peace offerings' and so on. These sacrifices were meant to be a response of love and obedience to God, rather than an attempt to stop him being angry, or even 'to keep on the

right side of God'. They were a special way God had
provided for his people to come to him, particularly
when they had done wrong.

Sacrifice has not been offered since the Temple was
destroyed in A.D. 70. The book of Hebrews shows that
the Old Testament sacrifices were not a complete answer
to the problem of human guilt and wrong-doing. Jesus'
sacrifice is seen as God's final answer for this.

THE *ARK. God gave Moses detailed instructions about
the making of the Ark (Exodus 25:10–22; 37:1–9). This
was a rectangular box made of acacia wood, some four
feet long, two and a half feet wide and two and a half feet
deep. The Ark represented God's throne—a visual aid
to remind the people that God was with them.

THE *COVENANT. The Ark contained the stone copies
of the Law given to Moses on Mount Sinai. This was the
Covenant, or special agreement made between God and
Israel, in which God promised to look after his people
and they promised to obey him.

THE *TABERNACLE. Instructions for making the
tabernacle were also given to Moses. It was a portable
tent, forty-five feet long, fifteen feet wide and fifteen feet
high. It was the place where the people worshipped until
the Temple was built.

THE *TEMPLE. This was only a small building some
eighty-seven feet long. It was first built by King Solomon
in the tenth century B.C. and the account of its building is
found in 1 Kings 6–8. It was destroyed by the Babylonians in 587 B.C., and rebuilt by Zerubbabel in 515 B.C.
and by Herod in 20 B.C. This last Temple was destroyed
by the Romans in A.D. 70. The Temple was the focal
point of Jewish worship in the Old Testament, and in the
New Testament times, when Jesus and his followers went
there to worship.

THE *SYNAGOGUE. We do not know how the synagogue first began. While the Jews were in exile in Babylon, without the Temple and its worship, they met
together to read and study the Law informally (Ezekiel
8:1; 14:1; 20:1). It is likely that the more organised and

formal synagogue worship arose out of this. In the New Testament period synagogues were found wherever there were Jews (as today). They were centres for the study of the Law, for worship (though without sacrifice), and for local government.

RELIGIOUS FESTIVALS AND HOLY DAYS

THE *SABBATH. Israel's most distinctive holy day was the Sabbath, or seventh day, which was to be kept separate from the rest of the week. It was a day when men and women were to rest, as God rested after making the world (Exodus 20:8–11). There were hot debates between Jesus and the religious leaders about what was allowed on the Sabbath, for there were many rules about what people could and could not do.

THE *PASSOVER. This was celebrated in mid-April, and is Israel's oldest and most distinctive festival. It celebrated the time when God delivered Israel from Egypt —the first Passover is described in Exodus 12. Every Jew would try to get to Jerusalem for Passover, but since the Temple was destroyed it has been celebrated at home. Jesus celebrated the Passover just before his death and gave it new meaning for Christians, as a celebration of their deliverance from guilt, sin and death.

*HARVEST FESTIVALS. There were several harvest festivals, the most important being:

Pentecost, which was seven weeks (50 days) after Passover, at the beginning of June. Pentecost celebrated the end of the grain harvest (wheat and barley), and the first sheaf of barley was offered to God. Later it also celebrated the giving of the Law. The Holy Spirit was given to the Church at Pentecost (Acts 2).

Feast of *Tabernacles was also called 'Ingathering'. It was six months after Passover, in mid-October, and celebrated the end of the vine and olive harvest. The people built shelters of branches (called 'booths'), as a reminder of the time when their ancestors had lived in tents in the desert before reaching Canaan.

THE DAY OF *ATONEMENT. This was the most

solemn of Israel's festivals and took place at the end of
September/beginning of October. It was a day when the
sin of the nation was confessed over a goat which was
then sent into the desert—a visual aid of the carrying
away of their sin.

The New Testament book of Hebrews links Jesus'
death with the Day of Atonement, showing that Jesus
has carried away the sin of his people.

*PURIM. This contrasts completely with the Day of
Atonement and is a day of fun and laughter. It celebrates
the Jewish deliverance from Haman through the intervention of Queen *Esther.

THE FEAST OF *DEDICATION. This is also called 'The
Festival of Lights' (John 10:22). It celebrates the exploits
of Judas Maccabeus in the second century B.C., when he
threw out the statue of the Greek god, Zeus, and re-
dedicated the Temple for the worship of God.

RELIGIOUS LEADERS

*PRIESTS. Aaron was Israel's first priest, and subsequent
priests were from his family. There are detailed instructions about the training and appointment of priests who
were 'set apart' (holy) for God's service. One of their
duties was to offer sacrifice, and they were the go-
between, between God and his people. In the book of
Hebrews Jesus is described as 'our great high priest'.

*SADDUCEES. This was a small, but very influential,
group of priests, who based their beliefs and practices on
the teachings of the Pentateuch. From the New Testament it is clear that they used the political situation for
their own ends, taking every opportunity to stay on the
right side of the Roman authorities. They were part of
the old-established upper class, and after the destruction
of the Temple the group went out of existence.

*PHARISEES. They appear very often in the New Testa-
ment, and were the largest group of religious leaders in
Jesus' day. We do not know how they began, but probably it was in the second century (the Maccabean period)
as protesters against Greek ideas. They were very con-

cerned about the correct and detailed keeping of the Law, as well as the many traditions associated with it.

*SCRIBES. Probably this group began in the reign of King David when they were 'court recorders' responsible for correspondence, state archives etc. During the exile in Babylon they became much more important because they not only taught and interpreted the Law, but also made sure it was passed on for future generations. *Ezra was both a priest and a scribe. In the New Testament they are referred to as 'teachers of the law' (*rabbis).

*PROPHETS. The first prophet was Samuel, but both Abraham and Moses are called prophets. They did speak about what would happen in the future, but much more of what they said was about moral, social and economic issues, and sometimes political and international matters as well. They were God's spokesmen, announcing what God had to say. Often this was not very comforting and so they were sometimes unpopular and even badly treated.

CHRISTIANITY AND BETWEEN THE TESTAMENTS

IN-BETWEEN EVENTS

There is no direct historical record of the four hundred years or so between the time of *Ezra–Nehemiah and the birth of Jesus. However, we learn about events from the history books of other nations as well as from the Apocrypha.

The Time Chart will show you the general pattern of events. The Persian empire fell to Alexander the Great of Greece and after his death his empire was divided between his four generals. In time two of these became important: the 'Ptolemaic' empire covering Egypt, and the 'Seleucid' empire, covering Syria and Mesopotamia. To begin with Israel was part of the Ptolemaic Empire but in 198 B.C. it passed into Seleucid control.

The period which followed is very important for Israel's history and is known as the **'Maccabean period'**. Jewish religion and culture was in danger of being stamped out by the Seleucid king, Antiochus IV (nicknamed 'Epiphanes', meaning 'God revealed'). Alexander the Great had begun a process called **'Hellenisation'**, that is, the spread of Greek culture throughout his empire, and his successors continued that process. Antiochus IV went too far, however. In the Temple at Jerusalem he set up a statue of the Greek god, Zeus, and then set about enforcing sacrifice to Greek gods in the towns and villages of Israel.

Many Jews had adopted Greek customs but many opposed the whole process. Opposition came to a head in the village of Modein where the Jewish priest Mattathias refused to offer sacrifice to a Greek god. He and his five sons fled to the hills and years of guerrilla warfare followed. His most famous son, Judas Maccabeus, eventually removed the statue of Zeus from the Temple, which he re-dedicated for the worship of God.

He and his family became the new leaders in Israel and in 142 B.C. Israel at last won its freedom. However, power

struggles among the descendants of the Maccabees eventually led to the intervention of Rome and in 63 B.C. Israel
became part of the Roman Empire. From now on, it was
governed by Jewish rulers approved and appointed by
Rome, of whom *Herod the Great, the Herod of Jesus'
birth (Matthew 2:1–18), was the best known.

THE APOCRYPHA

Some of the events between the end of the Old Testament
and the beginning of the New Testament are covered in a
number of additional books known together as the Apocrypha. Many Christians do not believe these books to be
part of the Holy Bible, although they may be useful for
reference. However, parts of the Christian Church, and in
particular Roman Catholics, do give these books the same
status as the rest of the Bible.

SIMILARITIES AND DIFFERENCES BETWEEN JEWISH AND CHRISTIAN BELIEFS

There are close links between Jewish religion and Christianity. At first, Christianity seemed to be a Jewish sect.
Christians worshipped in the Temple, went to the synagogue and celebrated the festivals. The New Testament
shows that just as the religious leaders had disagreed with
Jesus over many issues, so they disagreed with his followers. Eventually, Christianity was forced apart from Jewish
religion and became separate to it. Nevertheless, there are
many ideas which are found in both religions, and the
Jewish Scriptures—the Old Testament—are vital to our
understanding of the two.

*COVENANT (see also 'How the Bible was written' in
   the section 'How we got our Bible').

   The Old Testament is about the Old Covenant or
agreement, and the New Testament about the New
Covenant. The prophet Jeremiah had promised that one
day God would make this New Covenant (Jeremiah
31:31–34). Jesus refers to this chapter, and shows that his
death would bring this covenant into existence (Luke
22:20). Later, Paul says the same thing (2 Corinthians

3:6), and so does the writer to the Hebrews (8:8–12; 10:16).

The Old Covenant was made with the whole nation of Israel. The New Covenant was for Christians of all races. The Old Covenant was written on blocks of stone and contained rules which were to be obeyed. The New Covenant has the power to change the inner nature of men and women, and to give complete and lasting forgiveness.

*MESSIAH. The Jews looked forward to the time when God would send them a special leader who would lead them to victory over their enemies, and over the empires of which they were part. Many of their prophets spoke about this leader (e.g. Isaiah 9:2–7; 11:1–9), a man anointed by God (Messiah means 'anointed' in Hebrew; the Greek word 'Christ' means the same thing).

The New Testament shows us that the first Christians believed that Jesus was this promised Messiah. Matthew uses a formula many times to underline this belief: writing about the birth of Jesus for example, he says 'All this took place to fulfil what the Lord had said through the prophet . . .' (Matthew 1:22). In Acts the same point is made by the followers of Jesus who saw the resurrection as the evidence that Jesus was both the promised Messiah, and the Son of God (Acts 2:32, 36).

It was this belief, more than anything else, that caused the conflict between Jewish religion and Christianity. Jews believed that God 'was One', so how could Jesus be God? And if Jesus was God, how could God die? Yet Christian teachers insisted on this point and the belief in 'the Trinity' became part of the Christian creed: God the Father, God the Son and God the Holy Spirit.

The Holy Spirit appears in the Old Testament, coming to various people who needed special understanding or physical strength. In the New Testament Jesus speaks of the Holy Spirit as a person rather than as a 'force' (John 14:25–26; 16:7–11), and Paul shows that he gives special abilities to Christians (1 Corinthians 12:7–11).

SIMILARITIES AND DIFFERENCES BETWEEN JEWISH AND CHRISTIAN WORSHIP

It is clear that Christianity took over and developed some Jewish practices. To begin with Christians had only the Old Testament Scriptures, but their leaders would have spoken about the teachings of Jesus. As time went on, the writings which now form our New Testament would have been used in Christian worship. Indeed, we learn a lot from the New Testament about how the first Christians lived and worshipped—Acts 2:42, 46; 5:42; 1 Corinthians 11:20–34 for example.

THE CHRISTIAN SUNDAY. From the beginning Christians gathered together in various homes, as well as continuing to attend the synagogue and the Temple. Acts 2:46 tells us that they met together in the Temple each day, but in time 'the first day of the week' became the most important day for worship, since that was the day of Christ's resurrection (Acts 20:7; 1 Corinthians 16:2). It is called 'the Lord's Day' in Revelation 1:10.

The order of worship was probably based on the synagogue service. There are some simple 'creeds' (statements of belief) in the New Testament, and probably some early Christian songs (1 Corinthians 15:3–4; Ephesians 4:4–6; 1 Timothy 3:16). The Apostles' Creed, recited in some churches today, is a statement of the main points of Christian belief.

THE *LORD'S SUPPER. 1 Corinthians 11:17–34 is perhaps the earliest account of Christian worship. At the Last Supper Jesus gave new meaning to the Jewish *Passover, which had been a reminder of when God delivered his people from Egypt and a looking forward to the future kingdom of God.

The Lord's Supper (sometimes called 'The Eucharist', 'Holy Communion') is a reminder of Jesus' death, and a looking forward to his coming again. The bread, which had recalled the unleavened bread of the first Passover, becomes a reminder of the body of Jesus; the wine, a reminder of his blood, showing that he sacrificed his life so that men and women could be set free.

*BAPTISM. People who were not Jews and wanted to join the Jewish religion were baptised. John the Baptist baptised anyone (Jew or not) who wanted to make a new start and prepare themselves for the coming of Jesus.

Christians practised baptism from the first days of the Church—Jesus himself had been baptised. Wherever the gospel was preached converts were baptised (e.g. Acts 2:38, 41). Paul shows that baptism is a statement that a person intends to begin again—like Jesus who died and rose from the dead, they want to turn their back on the past and begin a new life (Romans 6:4).

SUMMARY. We see then, that Christianity's belief system has deep roots in Jewish religion and begins in the Old Testament:

God is the Creator of the world. He created men and women as a unique part of creation. But the human race has spoilt the basic design of God through disobedience and self-will. The human problem is the broken relationship with God, called *sin. The hope that this problem can be put right is only partially answered by the provision of *sacrifice. Sacrifice could provide a way for man to come to God but it could not change human nature.

The message which Christianity brings is that Jesus, the Son of God, who was present when God created the world, is the answer to the human problem. His death is a sacrifice which deals with human sin and guilt once and for all. His resurrection guarantees the resurrection of his followers. The Holy Spirit has been given to help men and women to live as God originally intended.

A BRIEF HISTORY OF ISRAEL

This section is intended to be used alongside the Time Chart. It will also be found useful to consult other sections and asterisks will indicate when more information is available in these.

THE BEGINNING OF TIME

In the section 'What is the Bible' and the paragraph 'A special kind of history' we saw that Biblical history focuses on events and people from a particular point of view, that is, 'how was God at work in this situation?' This is especially obvious in the first few chapters of Genesis.

They are often called 'Primeval History', that is to say, primitive history – the beginnings of human history. They tell us what happened before Israel even came on the scene: how the world began and the nations of the world emerged and how various languages and cultures evolved. Well-known characters (*Adam and *Eve, *Cain and *Abel, *Noah) appear in well-known stories (the *creation, the *fall and the *flood). Read Genesis 1–11.

FOUNDING FATHERS OF ISRAEL

*Abraham, his son *Isaac and grandson *Jacob were desert nomads. God spoke to Abraham and told him to leave the place where he lived (Mesopotamia) and travel to *Canaan. God promised that he would give him the land of Canaan and that he would become the ancestor of the nation of Israel.

Jacob had twelve sons whose names became the names of the twelve tribes which formed the nation of Israel. As a result of a severe famine in Canaan, Jacob and his twelve sons settled in Egypt. Read Genesis 12–50.

MOSES AND THE EXODUS

A change in the ruling family of Egypt resulted in the twelve tribes being oppressed. They were forced to work for the Egyptians as slaves and later all male babies were killed in an attempt to reduce the threat of rebellion. One baby, Moses, survived and was reared in the Egyptian palace. He had to withdraw into the desert after he had murdered an Egyptian but many years later God spoke to him and called him to lead the twelve tribes, which were to become the nation of Israel, out of Egypt. Despite the determined opposition of the Egyptian king's persistent refusal to Moses' request the people did leave Egypt and escaped into the desert area to the east of Egypt. Read Exodus 1–15.

ISRAEL BECOMES A NATION

After three months' journey the people came to the mountain called *Sinai and here Moses received the *Ten Commandments. A *covenant was made between God and the twelve tribes and from this point Israel becomes a nation. Read Exodus 16–20.

THE LAND OF CANAAN

Within a short time Israel could have settled into Canaan but they were too afraid of the tribes already living there and turned back into the desert where they lived and wandered for 38 years. By that time most of those who had left Egypt had died, including Moses. *Joshua had been chosen by God to lead Israel across the river Jordan into Canaan. Under his leadership various fortress towns, in particular *Jericho and Ai, were destroyed but the full occupation and possession of Canaan was a long, slow process. Read Joshua 1–11.

CONFEDERACY

After Joshua's death there was no one to act as a leader in Israel. In theory God was Israel's leader or king, but the people were very attracted by the nature religion of the tribes who lived in Canaan (worship of the gods such as *Baal) and were disloyal and disobedient to God. Moreover, they were constantly attacked by the many tribes who still lived in Canaan: *Ammonites, *Amalekites, Moabites, and in particular, *Philistines. From time to time they turned to God, asking for help against their enemies, and God sent them a leader (called a judge) who would gather an army to fight. Once the threat passed the people would gradually slip into their old ways. Read Judges.

FIRST KINGS

*Samuel was the last and greatest of these judges. At the time the Philistines were constantly attacking Israel and the people decided that they must have a king because they needed something more permanent than the random leadership of the judge-deliverers. God showed Samuel that he should allow Israel to have a king and led him to Saul from the tribe of Benjamin. As Israel's first king he turned out to be emotionally unstable and even before his death David, from the tribe of Judah, was chosen to succeed him. Read 1 Samuel 1–16.

DAVID AND SOLOMON

Saul spent the last few years of his reign trying to track down and kill David. There was civil war after Saul's death but eventually all the tribes of Israel united under David. David finally subdued the Philistines and Israel's boundaries extended further than ever before. Jerusalem was captured from the Canaanites (they called it Jebus) and it became the capital city of Israel. Towards the end of David's reign there was rivalry between his sons and consequent civil war, but *Solomon was chosen by David to succeed him. It was Solomon who built the *Temple in Jerusalem. Read 1 Samuel 31–2 Samuel 5 and 1 Kings 1–2.

DIVIDED KINGDOM

Although Solomon has a reputation for being wise the Bible shows that many of his policies created difficulties. In particular his building projects severely strained the economy, increasing taxes and forcing citizens to work for the state and do military service. The dissatisfaction this caused became clear after his death, when a delegation met with his son *Rehoboam to ask that he should change these unpopular policies. When Rehoboam not only refused but promised to make heavier demands ten tribes rebelled and formed a separate state under *Jeroboam, previously a civil servant in Solomon's government. These tribes were in the north of the land and became known as Israel or the Northern Kingdom. One of their early kings made *Samaria the capital of the Northern Kingdom. Read 1 Kings 12.

THE TWO KINGDOMS

The two tribes in the south were known as *Judah or the Southern Kingdom. Judah was more stable than Israel, particularly because it had a hereditary monarchy. The history of the Northern Kingdom is punctuated by coups and assassinations and rarely did more than two kings of the same family survive. Sometimes there was border fighting between North and South; sometimes, particularly under the threat of a common enemy, they were on friendly terms.

THE AGE OF THE PROPHETS

The history of both kingdoms is more-or-less downhill and depressing, at least in religious terms. The influence of the local nature religions remained strong and as the power of the ruling classes increased social inequality, oppression and injustice grew. God called men to speak out about these injustices and to remind his people of the laws and the promises of the covenant upon which the nation had been founded. *Elijah and *Elisha were the most notable in the earlier years of the Northern Kingdom. Read 1 Kings 17–19 and 2 Kings 2, 4–5.

GREAT NATIONS AND EMPIRES

Behind the scenes the powerful nation of *Assyria was quietly extending her empire. Although smaller nations such as *Syria, Israel and Judah combined to fight off the threat they were eventually overrun. The prophets spoke of this as God's judgment on his people's disobedience. They said that because of social injustice, the oppression of the weak and powerless, and worship which was hypocritical God was using Assyria to punish them. What they said is

recorded in detail in the books which bear their name:
Amos, Hosea, Micah and Isaiah.

THE END OF ISRAEL AND JUDAH

Assyria wiped out Israel and removed all the inhabitants to
various parts of the Assyrian empire. Although for a few
years Assyria laid seige to Jerusalem the Assyrian army
withdrew, leaving the city and its inhabitants to a further
hundred years of existence. Gradually Assyrian power
dwindled and was finally extinguished by *Babylon. This
meant that Judah now became part of the Babylonian
empire and soon the ruling and professional classes were
taken from Jerusalem to Babylon. A few years later Jerusalem, rebellious to the last, was razed to the ground and all
but a few of its inhabitants deported to Babylon. This was
the lowest point in Jewish Biblical history: the Temple, the
centre of its religion was in ruins, and without that and in a
place far from Israel it was questionable whether its culture
and religion could survive. Read 2 Kings 24–25.

THE PROPHETIC HOPE

As God's spokesmen had brought a message of judgment,
so now they brought a message of hope. That God would
bring back his people to the land of Israel after the time of
punishment was over had been hinted by most of the
prophets. *Jeremiah, and in particular *Ezekiel, looked
forward to the time when the Temple, the focal point for the
worship of God, would be rebuilt.

   Sure enough, the power of Babylon began to wane, as
had that of Assyria before her, and in 539 B.C. *Persia
conquered the city of *Babylon (an event spoken of in
Daniel 5) and the empire passed into Persian hands.
*Cyrus, the Persian king, issued a proclamation in the
following year which gave the Jews complete freedom to
return to Israel. Read Ezra 1:1–4.

RETURN

Within a few years small groups of Jews made the journey
back to Jerusalem, rebuilt the altar and laid the foundation

for a new temple. But people who lived in the area (*Samaritans, many of whom were descendants of the Northern Kingdom) were strongly opposed to the work and it ground to a halt. Two prophets, *Haggai and *Zechariah appeared on the scene to encourage the returned exiles and the Temple was completed in 515 B.C. Read Ezra 4–6.

SILENT INTERVAL

For the next 50 years we know little of the life of the new community, although the book of *Malachi suggests that it was disheartened and demoralised. Two men helped to change this situation: *Ezra, a teacher of the law, was sent to Jerusalem by the Persian king and *Nehemiah was given permission to leave his duties in the city of Susa to supervise the building of a wall round Jerusalem—so vital to keeping her enemies at bay. Social, economic and religious reforms helped to establish the new community and in particular they were reminded of the law and the covenant. Read Ezra 7–10 and Nehemiah.

IN-BETWEEN EVENTS

A summary of the period in between the Old and New Testaments is given in the section 'Christianity and between the Testaments'.

TO THE END OF THE NEW TESTAMENT PERIOD

The background of the New Testament is the Roman Empire. Roman emperors (caesars) are mentioned in connection with Jesus' birth (Augustus–Lk 2), his life and death (Tiberius–Lk 3:1), and in Acts 18:2 it is noted that Claudius expelled the Jews from Rome. We know that initially, opposition to Christianity came from the Jews, but as the New Testament period progresses it is clear that Rome became increasingly hostile. The emperor Nero (A.D. 54–68) certainly executed some Christians and there is a strong tradition that Peter was executed by him. Domitian (A.D. 81–96) organised a systematic persecution of Christians and this is strongly hinted at in the book of Revelation. In between all this, Jewish rebellion and unrest finally tried Roman patience beyond endurance. In A.D. 70 the Temple was destroyed under Titus, acting on orders from Emperor Vespasian. The Temple and its sacrifices finally ceased though Judaism is, of course, practised up to the present day.

TIME CHART

INTRODUCTORY NOTES

Over the last hundred years or so we have gained a better understanding of the history of the Jewish nation as it relates to world history. This is partly a result of the work of archaeologists combined with scientific ways of dating their discoveries. Thus we can be more accurate in dating biblical events.

Nevertheless, the further back into history we go the less is it possible to pinpoint a precise date. After about 1000 B.C. we can be more definite about dates, but before this (2000–1000 B.C.) there may be differences of up to 100 years. The dates marked with * on the chart below are those which are particularly debated although generally accepted. The abbreviation *c.* means 'about' (Latin 'circa'). ** means 'somewhere within this period'.

Surprisingly, it is harder to pinpoint many New Testament dates! The New Testament itself gives us fewer clues than the Old Testament about historical details. It is especially difficult to say precisely when many of the books were written, so all the dates in the chart are not the only dates suggested.

Biblical Period and where it is recorded   World Events

BEGINNINGS OF TIME Genesis

| | Middle Bronze Age |
| 2000 B.C. | 1950 – 1550 |

Abraham c. 2000 – 1825**
Isaac c. 1900 – 1725**
Jacob c. 1800 – 1700***
Joseph c. 1720 – 1550***
Jacob and his eleven sons join Joseph in Egypt c. 1700

EXODUS FROM EGYPT AND CONQUEST OF CANAAN Exodus – Joshua

| | Pharaoh Rameses II |
| 1300 B.C. | 1290 – 1224 |

Moses
Exodus 1280/1260*
Desert Wanderings
Joshua
Fall of Jericho 1240/1220*

DEATH OF JOSHUA TO THE FIRST KING Judges – 1 Samuel 12

| | PHILISTINES |
| 1200 B.C. | Iron Age |

Joshua 1300 – 1190*
The Judges 1220/1200 – 1050/1045
Samuel 1075 – 1035
Saul 1050/1045 – 1010

ISRAEL'S GOLDEN AGE 1 Samuel 13 – 1 Kings 11 (1 Chronicles 10 – 2 Chronicles 9)

| | PHILISTINES |
| 1000 B.C. | |

David 1010 – 970
Solomon 970 – 930

930 B.C.

800 B.C.

THE TWO KINGDOMS 1 Kings 12 – 2 Kings 17 (2 Chronicles 10 – 28)

Israel: The Northern Kingdom	Prophets	
930 – 909 Jeroboam I		
909 – 908 Nadab		
908 – 885 Baasha		
885 – 884 Elah		
884 Zimri		
884 Tibni		
884 – 873 Omri		
873 – 853 Ahab	Elijah	
853 – 852 Ahaziah		
852 – 841 Joram	Elisha	
841 – 813 Jehu	"	
813 – 798 Jehoahaz		
798 – 781 Jehoash	? Jonah	
781 – 753 Jeroboam II	Amos c. 760 – 750	
753 – 752 Zechariah	Hosea c. 750 – 725	
752 Shallum		
752 – 741 Menahem	"	Tiglath Pileser III of ASSYRIA 745 – 727
741 – 739 Pekahiah	"	
739 – 731 Pekah	"	
731 – 722 Hoshea	"	Shalmanezer V of ASSYRIA 727 – 722
Fall of Samaria, capital of Israel 722		

930 B.C.

800 B.C.

700 B.C.

600 B.C.

Judah: The Southern Kingdom	Prophets
930 – 913 Rehoboam	
913 – 910 Abijah	
910 – 869 Asa	
869 – 848 Jehoshaphat	
848 – 841 Jehoram	
841 Ahaziah	
841 – 835 Athaliah	
835 – 796 Joash	
796 – 767 Amaziah	
767 – 739 Azariah (Uzziah)	Isaiah 740 – 701
739 – 731 Jotham	"
731 – 715 Ahaz	Micah 725 – 701

Tiglath Pileser III
of ASSYRIA 745 – 727
Shalmanezer V of
ASSYRIA 727 – 722

→

LAST DAYS OF JUDAH 1 Kings 18 – 25 (2 Chronicles 29 – 36)

Judah	Prophets	
715 – 686 Hezekiah	Isaiah/Micah	Sennacherib of ASSYRIA
710 Siege of Jerusalem		
686 – 641 Manasseh		
641 – 639 Amon		Fall of Nineveh, capital of ASSYRIA 612
639 – 609 Josiah	Jeremiah/?Zephaniah/?Jonah ?Nahum/?Habakkuk/?Joel Lamentations	
609 Jehoahaz		
609 – 597 Jehoiakim		Nebuchadnezzar of BABYLON
605 Daniel deported to Babylon		
597 Jehoiachin	Ezekiel 593 – 571	
'First' deportation to Babylon		
597 – 587 Zedekiah	Obadiah	
'Second' deportation to Babylon		

500 B.C.

300 B.C.

200 B.C.

100 B.C.

EXILE AND RETURN Ezra, Nehemiah, Esther, Haggai, Zechariah, Malachi, Isaiah 40 – 66

		Prophets
		Cyrus of PERSIA
		Artaxerxes of PERSIA
539	Fall of Babylon	
538	Cyrus' Decree	
	First Return to Jerusalem	
515	Dedication of second Jerusalem temple	Haggai 520
		Zechariah 520
		Malachi c.500 – 450
445	Nehemiah arrives in Jerusalem	
428**	Ezra arrives in Jerusalem	

BETWEEN THE TESTAMENTS (1 & 2 Maccabees, in the APOCRYPHA)

Fall of PERSIA 331

Antiochus Epiphanes,
SELEUCID king 175 – 163

336 – 323	Alexander the Great of GREECE
323	Greek Empire divided into Ptolemaic (Egypt) and Seleucid (Syria and Mesopotamia)
323 – 198	Israel a Ptolemaic state
198 – 166	Israel a Seleucid state
167	Desecration of Jerusalem temple
	Maccabean Revolt
165	Jerusalem temple rededicated
142	Jewish Independence
63	Pompey of Rome annexes Jerusalem
40 B.C. – 4 A.D.	Herod the Great

LIFE OF JESUS Matthew, Mark, Luke, John

?4 B.C.	Birth of John the Baptist
?4	Birth of Jesus
?29 A.D.	Baptism of Jesus
30/33 A.D.	Crucifixion

27 B.C. – 14 A.D. Caesar Augustus of ROME

26 – 30 A.D. Pontius Pilate

30 A.D.

THE EARLY CHURCH Acts & Letters

		Literature	
35	Paul's conversion	49/50	Galatians
47	Paul's first missionary journey	50 – 51	1 & 2 Thessalonians
49	Important Church Council	55 – 56	1 & 2 Corinthians
50 – 52	Paul's second missionary journey	58	Romans
		**50 – 62	James
		61	Philemon, Colossians, Ephesians Philippians
53 – 57	Paul's third missionary journey		
64	Death of Paul in Rome	62	1 Peter
70	Fall of Jerusalem to Rome	**62 – 64	1 & 2 Timothy, Titus
		**63/64	Mark
		64 – 68	2 Peter
		**65 – 68	Hebrews
		70	Matthew
		80	Jude
		**65 – 80	Luke, Acts
		**75 – 85	John
		**70 – 100	1,2,3, John
		**90 – 100	Revelation
		**90 – 95	

41 – 54 Claudius

54 – 68 Nero

81 – 96 Domitian

50 A.D.

100 A.D.

MAPS

Map 1

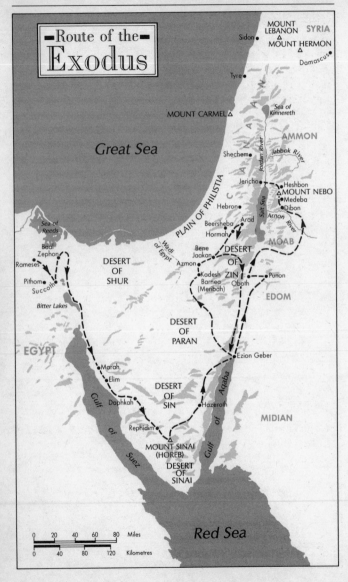

Route of the Exodus

Great Sea

Red Sea

Map 2

71

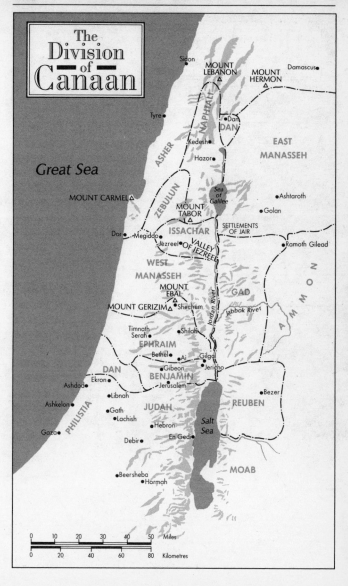

The
Division
of
Canaan

Great Sea

Sidon

MOUNT
LEBANON

MOUNT
HERMON

Damascus

Tyre

NAPHTALI

Dan

DAN

EAST
MANASSEH

Kedesh

ASHER

Hazor

Ashtaroth

MOUNT CARMEL

ZEBULUN

Sea of
Galilee

Golan

MOUNT
TABOR

ISSACHAR

SETTLEMENTS
OF JAIR

Dor

Megiddo

Jezreel

VALLEY
OF JEZREEL

Ramoth Gilead

WEST
MANASSEH

MOUNT
EBAL

AMMON

MOUNT GERIZIM

Shechem

Jordan River

GAD

Jabbok River

Timnath
Serah

Shiloh

EPHRAIM

Bethel

Ai

Gilgal

DAN

Gibeon

Jericho

Ashdod

Ekron

BENJAMIN

Jerusalem

Bezer

Ashkelon

Libnah

JUDAH

REUBEN

Gath

Lachish

Gaza

PHILISTIA

Hebron

Salt
Sea

Debir

En Gedi

MOAB

Beersheba

Hormah

| 0 | 10 | 20 | 30 | 40 | 50 | Miles |
| 0 | 20 | 40 | 60 | 80 | | Kilometres |

The Holy Land at the time of Jesus

Mediterranean Sea

PHOENICIA

SYRIA

Sidon

Damascus

MOUNT HERMON

Tyre

Caesarea Philippi

Ptolemais

GALILEE

Chorazin
Bethsaida
Capernaum
Cana
Magadan
Sea of Galilee
MOUNT CARMEL
Nazareth
Tiberias
Nain
Gadara

Caesarea

Pella

DECAPOLIS

Sebaste (Samaria)
Shechem
Sychar

SAMARIA

River Jordan

Joppa

Arimathea

Ephraim

PEREA

Philadelphia

Jamnia
Emmaus

Jericho

Azotus

Jerusalem
Bethany
Bethlehem

Ashkelon

JUDEA

Salt Sea (Dead Sea)

Gaza

Hebron

IDUMEA

Beersheba

NABATEA

0   10   20   30   40 Miles
0   20   40   60 Kilometres

Map 4   73

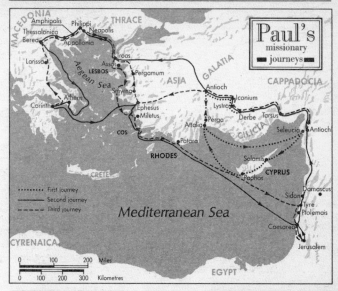

BIBLE INDEX

AARON Born in Egypt, he assisted his younger brother, **Moses**, in arranging for the release of the Israelite people from Egypt (Ex 4:27ff). After their release he became the first **high priest** of Israel (Ex 28–29) and his male descendants (the 'house of Aaron') became official priests (Lev 8; Ps 115:12).

ABADDON (destruction). The Hebrew name of the evil angel (Rev 9:11) who reigns over the **Abyss** (the place of departed spirits). Also called in Greek, **Apollyon**.

ABBA An Aramaic word. A child's familiar name for 'father'; used by Jesus when addressing his Father and by Christians when addressing God in personal prayer (Mk 14:36; Ro 8:15; Gal 4:6).

ABEDNEGO (servant of Nego). The adopted name of Azariah, a Jewish exile in Babylon (Da 1:7). Here he served as an administrator along with **Shadrach** and **Meshach**. All three were cast into a blazing furnace but were miraculously saved (Da 3:12–20).

ABEL (breath). The second son of **Adam** and **Eve**. He was murdered by his jealous brother, **Cain** (Ge 4; Heb 11:4). Regarded as the first martyr and model of righteousness (Mt 23:35; Lk 11:51).

ABIATHAR (excellent father). A priest who escaped a massacre at Nob (1 Sa 22:11–23). With **Zadok** he served King **David** as joint **high priest**: as such he accompanied the **Ark** to Jerusalem, when David made it the capital city (1 Ch 15:11f). He was deposed by King **Solomon** for supporting Adonijah's attempt to succeed David (1 Ki 1–2).

ABIGAIL (source of joy). (1) Wife of Nabal (1 Sa 25:3), she persuaded King **David** not to avenge her husband's insult and on Nabal's death she married David (1 Sa 25:42).

She shared his adventures at Gath and Ziklah (1 Sa 27:3; 30:5) and bore him a son at Hebron (2 Sa 3:3). (2) A sister or step-sister of David (2 Sa 17:25; 1 Ch 2:13–17) and mother of Amasa, an army commander (1 Ch 2:17).

ABIJAH (Yahweh is my father). The name of one woman (2 Ch 29:1) and eight men (1 Ch 2:24; 7:8; 1 Sa 8:2; 1 Ch 24:10 & Lk 1:5; 1 Ki 14:1–18; 2 Ch 12:16ff; Ne 12:4; 10:7). Of these the most important is the king of Judah, son and successor of **Rehoboam** 913–911 B.C. (1 Ki 14:31–15:8; 2 Ch 12:16–14:1).

ABIMELECH (my father is king). (1) The name of two Philistine kings of Gerar, both of whom made treaties with patriarchs—with **Abraham** (Ge 20) and **Isaac** (Ge 26). (2) The son of **Gideon** (Jdg 8:31). After his father's death, he slew seventy sons of his father and was made king of Shechem. Here he cruelly put down a rebellion before meeting his own death as he attacked Thebez (Jdg 9).

ABNER (father of light). Cousin of King **Saul** and commander-in-chief of the army (1 Sa 14:50). He brought **David** to Saul after the slaying of Goliath (1 Sa 17:55–58). Following Saul's death he supported Ishbosheth's claim to the throne but afterwards went over to David (2 Sa 3:6f). Murdered by the jealous **Joab** (2 Sa 3:27) and mourned by David (1 Sa 3:33–34).

ABOMINATION **Daniel** spoke of some future notable and frightful desecration of the Temple of Jerusalem (Da 9:27; 11:31; 12:11); and Jesus also warned of an abomination that causes desolation occurring before the end of the age (Mt 24:14; Mk 13:14). Possibly Daniel's prophecy was fulfilled when an altar to Zeus was placed in the Temple in 167 B.C. and that of Jesus when the Roman armies sacked Jerusalem in A.D. 70.

ABRAHAM (father of multitudes). Ancestor of several nations, particularly the Hebrew (Ge 17:5). Born at **Ur of**

the Chaldees, he married Sarai, later moving to Haran, where his father, Terah, died (Ge 11:27–32). Responding to God's call he journeyed to Canaan, a land which God promised to give to him and his descendants (Ge 12). Although both he and his wife were aged and childless, a son, **Isaac**, was miraculously conceived and born to them (Ge 15). Abraham's faith was severely tested when God ordered him to sacrifice his son at Moriah: but his willingness to obey resulted in Isaac being delivered and a ram being substituted (Ge 22). The faith of this patriarch of the Israelites is used by the apostle **Paul** to illustrate how a believer is in a right relationship with God (Ro 4).

ABSALOM (father of peace). Handsome son of King **David** and Maacah (2 Sa 3:3; 14:25–27). He killed Amnon for raping his sister, Tamar, and was then banished by David (2 Sa 13). On his return he led a rebellion against his father, posing a very serious threat to the throne (2 Sa 15). Against David's wishes he was killed by loyal soldiers and this led the king to excessive grief (2 Sa 18–19:8).

ABYSS The place where God causes evil spirits to dwell (Lk 8:31) and where, also, the disobedient spirits of the departed are held (Rev 9:1–2; 20:1–3). Sometimes this was thought of as being in the depths of the earth.

ACHAN An Israelite who disobeyed **Joshua** and took booty from **Jericho**, when the booty had been dedicated to the LORD (Jos 6: 17–19). His disobedience brought defeat for Israel at Ai. After being found out, he was stoned to death and cremated in a valley consequently named Achor (Jos 7).

ADAM (of the ground). Both a personal name and a general noun meaning mankind. The name of the first man formed by God of the dust of the ground as the climax of his **creation** (Ge 1:26; 2:7; Lk 3:38). His disobedience (**fall**) to God's command led to the expulsion from the garden of Eden (Ge 3). He died aged 930 (Ge 5:5). Paul draws a contrast between Christ and Adam as two representative men (1 Co 15:22, 45; Ro 5:12–15). And Jesus used Adam's union with **Eve** to illustrate the permanent nature of marriage (Mt 19:4–6).

ADONIJAH (my Lord is Yahweh). Fourth son of King **David**, who tried to seize the kingdom with the support of **Joab**, the army commander and **Abiathar**, the high priest. He surrendered to Solomon, but was later accused of treason and executed (1 Ki 1:5–2:28).

ADULTERY In the OT the sexual intercourse between a man (married or unmarried) and the wife of another: forbidden by God's commandment (Ex 20:14; Dt 5:18). The normal punishment for the guilty was death by stoning (Dt 22:22–24). Also it was used figuratively of the forsaking of the worship of the LORD for false gods (Isa 57:3; Jer 3:8–9; Eze 23:37, 43; Hos 2:4; 4:15).

Jesus broadened the commandment to include the lustful look of an adulterous heart (Mt 15:19; Mk 7:21). He taught that remarriage of a divorcee was adultery (Mt 5:31–32; 19:3–9; Mk 10:2–12; Lk 16:18), and he used adultery figuratively of unfaithfulness to God (Mt 12:39; 16:4; Mk 8:38).

AGE Either the period of time from the birth of Christ to the end of the world (Mk 10:30; Ro 12:2; 2 Ti 4:10; Tit 2:12) or the period after the end of the world which has no ending (Mt 12:32; Eph 1:21; Heb 6:5). The great event between the two ages is the second coming of Christ to judge the world (Mt 13:39).

AGRIPPA (1) Agrippa I son of Aristobulus and grandson of **Herod** the Great. He is called Herod in Acts 12. From A.D. 40 till his death in 44 he ruled over Judea and Samaria, under the Roman Empire. (2) Agrippa II was his son and was the ruler over Iturea, Trachonitis and Abilene when **Paul** appeared before him (Ac 25:23–26:32) seeking to convert him to Christ. He died in A.D. 100 in Rome.

AHAB (father's brother). Son of **Omri** and seventh king of the northern kingdom of Israel (874–852 B.C.). He married the pagan **Jezebel**, princess of Sidon, and built a temple for her dedicated to her god, **Baal** of Tyre (1 Ki 16:32). As a result Ahab had to contend with the prophet **Elijah** throughout his reign (1 Ki 17–22). In war Ahab conquered the Syrians (1 Ki 20:21) but was condemned for sparing their king, Ben-Hadad (1 Ki 20:42). Urged on by Jezebel, Ahab seized Naboth's vineyard (1 Ki 21) and earned a sentence of judgment from Elijah. Then, misled by false prophets, Ahab met his death fighting against the Syrians (1 Ki 22:34–38).

AHAZ (possessor). Succeeded his father, **Jotham**, as king of Judah (735–715 B.C.). His army suffered heavily through an invasion by Israel and Syria. Ahaz refused to respond to the prophet Isaiah's appeal for trust in the LORD (Isa 7), and turned to Tiglath-Pileser of **Assyria** for help (2 Ki 16:7). This led to a century in which Judah was a mere dependant of Assyria as well as to the erection of a pagan altar in the Temple of Jerusalem (2 Ki 16:10ff).

AHAZIAH (Yahweh has grasped). (1) Son and successor of **Ahab**, king of Israel. Reigned only two years and was condemned by **Elijah** for worshipping the pagan god of Ekron (1 Ki 22:51–52; 2 Ki 1:1–18). (2) Youngest son of **Jehoram** and king of Judah, whose brief reign of one year is described as evil (2 Ch 22:3). He was slain by **Jehu** (2 Ki 9:16–28).

AHIJAH (Yahweh is my brother). A prophet of **Shiloh**, who tore a new robe into twelve pieces, ten of which he gave to **Jeroboam**. This symbolised the division of Solomon's kingdom into **Judah** and **Israel** (1 Ki 11:26–40). And when Jeroboam led Israel into idolatry he foretold the extinction of his family (1 Ki 14:6–16).

AHITHOPHEL An adviser of King **David** (2 Sa 16:23) who conspired with **Absalom**. When his advice was not followed

he foresaw the collapse of the rebellion and hanged himself
(2 Sa 17).

AI (ruin). A small city of central Palestine, east of Bethel.
It was the second Canaanite city taken by **Joshua** and is
particularly linked with the sin of Achan (Jos 7–8). Later
occupied by members of the tribe of Benjamin (Ne 7:32).

ALEXANDRIA Seaport founded by Alexander the Great
in 332 B.C. when he conquered Egypt (Ac 27:6; 28:11).
It became a centre of learning. **Apollos** came from here
(Ac 18:24).

ALLELUIA See **Hallelujah**.

ALMIGHTY The expression 'God Almighty' or 'LORD
Almighty' occurs many times in the OT, and a few times in
the NT. God is all-powerful but that power is in accordance
with his holy love. See Ge 17:1; 43:14; Ps 46:7, 11; Isa 1:9,
24; Jer 6:6, 9; Mal 1:4, 6, 8, 9; Rev 1:8; 4:8; 21; 22.

ALPHA The first letter of the Greek alphabet, thus pointing to the beginning or origin of a thing. Used of Christ
figuratively (Rev 1:8; 21:6; 22:13).

ALTAR A place of meeting with God where a gift is offered
to him by way of a sacrifice. The first Hebrew altar of which
we read was erected by Noah (Ge 8:20): later, altars were
erected by Abraham (Ge 12:7; 13:4; 22:9), Isaac (26:25),
Jacob (35:1–7) and Moses (Ex 17:15).

  With the creation of the **tabernacle** two altars were built
for the regular worship of the Israelites: an altar of **burnt-
offering** (Ex 25:9) and of **incense** (Ex 30:1). Both also were
found in the later Temple in Jerusalem (2 Ch 4:1ff).

  The Christian Church as described in the NT had no
altars or use for them since Jesus' sacrifice on the cross was
seen as the end of all the OT sacrifices (Heb 10).

AMALEK (valley dweller). Son of Eliphaz, grandson of

Esau (Ge 36:12, 16). Name also used collectively of his descendants (Ex 17:8).

AMALEKITES Nomadic Arabian tribe, descendants of **Amalek**, living in the desert south of Judah. They constantly opposed the Israelites in the days of **Moses** (Ex 17:8), **Gideon** (Jdg 7:12), **Samuel** and **Saul** (1 Sa 14:48), **David** (1 Sa 27:8) and **Hezekiah** (1 Ch 4:43).

AMAZIAH (Yahweh is strong). (1) Son and successor of **Jehoash** as king of Judah 796–767 B.C. Over-confident after a great victory over **Edom** (2 Ki 14:7), he attacked **Jehoash** of Israel and suffered a disastrous defeat and he was captured (2 Ki 14:13). (2) A priest of **Jeroboam II** of Israel who tried to silence the prophet, Amos, at Bethel (Am 7:10).

AMEN (truly). A term signifying the agreement and acceptance by a worshipper of that which has been stated (Dt 27:15–26; 1 Ki 1:36; 1 Ch 16:36; Ps 41:13; 72:19; 1 Co 14:16; Rev 1:6–7; 3:14).

AMMON/AMMONITES Descendants of Ben-Ammi, Lot's younger son by his daughter (Ge 19:38). They were therefore to be treated as relatives by the Israelites but they proved lasting enemies (Dt 2:19). They were constantly at war with Israel (Jdg 3:13; 10:7; 2 Ch 20) and were often condemned by the prophets (Jer 49:1; Eze 25:2; Am 1:13; Zep 2:8).

AMON (master workman). (1) Son and successor of **Manasseh** as king of Judah (642–640 B.C.). His brief and idolatrous reign was cut short by a palace revolution (2 Ki 21:18–26). (2) Governor of Samaria charged by King Ahaz to hold the prophet **Micaiah** when the king went to battle (1 Ki 22:26). (3) Egyptian god whose temple was at Thebes (also called No) (Jer 46:25).

AMORITES (mountain-dwellers). Descendants of Canaan (Ge 10:16) they were a prominent people in and around

Palestine before the arrival of **Joshua** and the tribes of Israel (Ge 15:16; Dt 20:17; Jos 3:10; Ex 33:2). Israel's occupation of the land began with the overthrow of the Amorite kings Sihon of Heshbon and Og of Bashan (Jos 12). The Amorites were gradually absorbed (1 Ki 9:20) but memories of their idolatry lingered (1 Ki 21:26; 2 Ki 21:11).

AMOS (burdened). Shepherd and cultivator of sycamore-fig trees (Am 7:14), a native of Tekoa, near Jerusalem. God called him to prophesy in the reigns of **Uzziah** of Judah and **Jeroboam II** of Israel—760 B.C.: wrote book of Amos in the OT.

ANANIAS (Yahweh has been gracious). (1) A Christian in **Jerusalem** who collapsed and died when his deceit was exposed (Ac 5:1). (2) A Christian in Damascus who ministered to the newly-converted **Saul** of Tarsus (Ac 9:10). (3) The high priest before whom **Paul** was tried (Ac 23:2; 24:1) and by whom Paul was referred to the Roman ruler, **Felix**.

ANCIENT OF DAYS Title given to God as Judge of the world in the book of Daniel (7:9, 13, 22). It suggested comfort for God's people through his unsurpassable wisdom and pure integrity when dealing with human affairs.

ANDREW (manly). **Apostle** of Jesus (Mt 10:2). From Bethsaida in Galilee (Jn 1:44) he went to live at **Capernaum** (Mk 1:29) in a fishing partnership with **Peter** (Mt 4:18). He was pointed to Jesus by **John the Baptist** (Jn 1:35–40) and in turn he introduced his brother to Jesus (Jn 1:42). He is mentioned with reference to the ministry of Jesus (Jn 6:8; 12:22; Mk 13:3) and was present at the **Ascension** (Ac 1:13).

ANGEL (messenger). A supernatural, heavenly being (Ps 148:2–5; Heb 1:14). Angels are in God's presence to worship him (Heb 1:6; Rev 5:11) and are also sent into space and time as God's messengers (Ge 19:1; Ps 91:11; Da

3:28). They were particularly associated with the ministry of Jesus (Lk 2:9ff; Mt 4:11; 28:2; Lk 22:43; Ac 1:10–11).

There are evil angels whose leader is the **devil** or **Satan** (2 Pe 2:4; Jude 6).

ANGEL OF THE CHURCH Either a guardian angel or an angelic pastor (Rev 2:1, 8, 12, 18; 3:1, 7, 14).

ANGEL OF THE LORD In the OT the special (perhaps unique) messenger of God whose holy presence seems to be that of God himself (Ge 16:7–14; 22:11–18; Ex 3:2–5; 1 Ch 21:15–17). In the NT Gabriel is apparently this messenger (Lk 1:19).

ANNA (grace). An aged widow of the tribe of Asher who welcomed the baby Jesus as the long-awaited Messiah (Lk 2:36–38).

ANOINTING Applying oil to the human body was a common procedure both in life (Ru 3:3; Ps 104:15; Lk 7:46) and at death (Mk 14:8; 16:1). There was also sacred anointing to dedicate a person or thing to the Lord. The **Tabernacle** and its furniture (Ex 20:22ff), **prophets** (1 Ki 19:16), **priests** (Ex 28:41) and kings (1 Sa 16:1,12–13) were anointed. 'The Lord's anointed' was the king (1 Sa 12:3) and this term (= **Messiah**) was used in the OT for the future deliverer (Ps 2:2; Da 9:25–26) and in the NT of Jesus, anointed by the **Holy Spirit** (Jn 1:32–33; Lk 4:18, 21).

ANTICHRIST (one against Christ). Opponent of Christ in the last days of this age (1 Jn 2:18, 22; 4:3; 2 Jn 7).

ANTIOCH Sixteen cities of this name were founded by Seleucus I Nicator (358–280 B.C.). Two are mentioned in the NT. (1) Antioch of Pisidia in Phrygia of Asia Minor (Ac 13:14). (2) Antioch on the Orontes, 300 miles north of Jerusalem, capital of the province of Syria and third largest city of the Roman Empire. The church here had an important role in the outward mission to the Gentile nations (Ac 11 & 15).

APOLLOS A Jew from Alexandria who was instructed in knowledge of Jesus by **Aquila** and **Priscilla** (Ac 18:24–26). He then preached Jesus to fellow Jews (Ac 18:27–28) and at Corinth a group of converts even took his name (1 Cor 1:12).

APOLLYON (destroyer). Greek equivalent of **Abaddon**, angel of the **Abyss** (Rev 9:11).

APOSTLE (sent one). Applied in the NT both to Jesus (Heb 3:1) and to God's messengers to Israel (Lk 11:49); but usually to the twelve disciples who were commissioned by Jesus (Mt 10:2; Mk 3:13; Lk 6:13; Ac 1:13) and to **Paul** (Ro 1:1).

AQUILA AND PRISCILLA A Jewish-Christian couple who were expelled from Rome in A.D. 49. They entertained **Paul** at Corinth (Ac 18:1–3), risked their lives for him (Ro 16:3) and went with him to **Ephesus**, where they helped **Apollos** to a deeper faith (Ac 18:18ff).

ARAM; ARAMEANS; ARAMAIC Aram was the area north of Israel and eastwards to Mesopotamia (= Syria) (Nu 23:7; 2 Sa 8:6; 15:8; 1 Ch 2:23; Hos 12:12). Aramaic was a Semitic language in a variety of dialects and closely related to Hebrew: spoken by Arameans from 3000 B.C., and spoken in Palestine at the time of Jesus (2 Ki 18:26; Ezr 4:7; Da 2:4; Ac 21:40; 22:2).

ARARAT A mountainous district of later Armenia, where Noah's ark came to rest (Ge 8:4). The land to which Adrammelech and Sharezer fled (2 Ki 19:37) and summoned by **Jeremiah** to join in destroying **Babylon** (Jer 51:27).

ARCHANGEL A chief **angel**, whose voice signals the raising of the dead at the end of the age (1 Th 4:16). Named as Michael (Jude 9).

ARCHELAUS The eldest son of **Herod** the Great; he succeeded his father in 4 B.C. but without the title of king (Mt 2:22). He was exiled by the Romans in A.D. 6.

AREOPAGUS (hill of Ares). The ancient and prestigious court of **Athens**, named after its original meeting place on the hill of Ares (= Mars' hill). **Paul** appeared before this court (Ac 17:19ff).

ARK, NOAH'S A vessel of gopher wood, reeds and bitumen, built according to divine instructions for the preservation of Noah and his family together with a selection of animals from the Flood (Ge 6–9; Heb 11:7; 1 Pe 3:20).

ARK OF THE TESTIMONY (chest of the covenant). A rectangular box of acacia wood, covered with gold; its lid (called mercy seat) was of solid gold surmounted by two cherubs with outstretched wings. Details for its construction were given by God to **Moses** (Ex 25) and carried out by Bezalel (Ex 37:1). It contained the tablets of the written **Law**, a pot of manna and **Aaron's** rod (Heb 9:4) and rested first in the **Tabernacle** and later in the **Temple**. It was carried before the people in the wilderness (Nu 10:33) and as they entered Palestine (Jos 3; 4:7–11). **David** had it brought to Jerusalem and it went into Solomon's Temple (2 Sa 6; 1 Ch 13,15; 1 Ki 8:3–9). After the destruction of this Temple it disappeared for ever.

ARMOUR There are descriptions of ancient armour as worn by **Goliath** (1 Sa 17:4–7) and **Saul** (1 Sa 17:38; 31:9–10) and of Roman armour as seen by Paul (Eph 6:11–18).

ARMY Before the unification of the nation of Israel under the kings, armies were raised only to meet emergencies (Jdg 3:28; 4:6). King **Saul** organised the first regular Israelite army (1 Sa 13:2; 14:52) and this was developed by **David** (2 Sa 23:8–39) and **Solomon** (1 Ki 4:26).

ARTEMIS (= Diana). The Greek goddess of the moon,

daughter of Jupiter, twin sister of Apollo. Her special worship was centred in the great temple at Ephesus (Ac 19:24–35), which was one of the seven wonders of the world.

ASA (healer). King of Judah (911–870 B.C.) whose reforming zeal abolished idolatry and cultic prostitution (1 Ki 15–16; 2 Ch 14–16). His reforms began by his removal of his grandmother, Maacah, who worshipped idols (2 Ch 15:16).

ASAPH (collector). David made him choirmaster in Jerusalem (1 Ch 16:5) and his descendants continued to direct the music (1 Ch 25; 2 Ch 20:14; 35:15). Author of psalms used by Hezekiah in the revised Temple worship (Ps 50, 73–83).

ASCENSION The final appearance of the resurrected Jesus to his disciples, forty days after his resurrection. From Mount Olivet he went up and was received into a cloud, having previously commissioned his disciples to take the Gospel into the whole world (Ac 1:9; Lk 24:51; Mk 16:19).

ASHER (happy). Eighth son of **Jacob** by Leah's maid, Zilpah (Ge 30:13; 35:26); he had four sons and a daughter (Ge 46:17; Nu 26:46). The prosperity of his descendants (1 Ch 7:30ff) was prophesied in the last blessing of **Jacob** (Ge 49:20) and **Moses** (Dt 33:24). Those descendants formed the tribe of Israel of the same name (Nu 26:44–47; Jos 19:24–31, 34; Jdg 1:31–32). The aged prophetess, **Anna**, was of this tribe (Lk 2:36).

ASHERAH A Canaanite mother-goddess, associated with **Baal** (Jdg 3:7) and also the name of an image representing the goddess (1 Ki 15:13). Israelites were commanded to destroy these images (Dt 12:3; Ex 34:13).

ASHES In connection with sackcloth, powdery ashes were a symbol of mourning (2 Sa 13:19; Est 4:3; Isa 58:5).

ASHTAROTH, ASHTORETH A Canaanite mother-goddess associated with fertility, love and war (1 Ki 11:5). Israelites often turned from **Yahweh** to this goddess (Jdg 2:13; 10:6; 1 Sa 7:3–4; 12:10) and the cult of worship was even given royal approval by **Solomon** (1 Ki 11:5; 2 Ki 23:13).

ASIA As used in NT times, not modern Asia but the Roman province which covered the west of Asia Minor. The major cities were **Ephesus**, Smyrna (modern Izmir) and Pergamum. **Paul** travelled here (Ac 16:6; 19:10ff) and seven churches of Asia are mentioned in Rev 1–3.

ASSEMBLY In the OT the sacred assembly is the coming together of the tribes of Israel to meet the LORD (Ex 12:16; Lev 19:2; 23:7; Nu 10:7; Dt 31:30; 1 Ki 8:5; 1 Ch 13:2).

ASSYRIA, ASSYRIANS See page 42.

ATHALIAH (Yahweh is exalted). The only woman who ruled over Judah (841–835 B.C.; 2 Ki 8:18, 25–28; 11:1–20; 2 Ch 22:1–23:21). Daughter of **Ahab** and **Jezebel**.

ATHENS Self-governing Greek city, linked to Rome by special treaty. Paul addressed the **Areopagus** here and proclaimed Jesus as Lord (Ac 17:15–34; 1 Th 3:1).

ATONEMENT, DAY OF On the 10th day of the 7th month (Tishri) Israelites held their most solemn holy day, when a strict fast was kept. The details of what happened are given in Lev 16. The purpose of the **sacrifice** of the bullock and he-goat, the sprinkling of their blood, and the sending of another goat out into the wilderness, was to bring reconciliation between the gracious God and the confessing sinner. A Christian interpretation with reference to the atonement made by Christ is given in Heb 9–10.

AUGUSTUS (worthy of worship). Additional name conferred by the Roman Senate in 27 B.C. on Caesar Octavian

(63 B.C.–A.D. 14). Jesus was born at the time of the census he ordered (Lk 2:1).

AZARIAH (Yahweh has helped). The name of 25 different men in the OT, among whom is King Azariah of Judah (767–740 B.C.), also called **Uzziah** (2 Ki 14:21–22; 15:1–7; 2 Ch 26).

BAAL (owner, lord, husband). OT term for Canaanite nature and fertility gods of which Hadad, the storm god, was most important. The Baal challenged by **Elijah** on Mt Carmel was Melqart, god of Tyre (1 Ki 18). **Asherah** and **Ashtaroth** occur as the name of female deities who consort with Baal (Jdg 2:13; 3:7). Israel's worship, given the religious context, was constantly infected by ideas and ritual from the Baal cults and this was condemned by the prophets (Nu 25:3; Jer 7:9; Hos 2:8; Zep 1:4).

BAASHA (boldness). He became the third king of Israel (909–885 B.C.) by assassinating Nadab and eliminating the house of **Jeroboam** (1 Ki 15:16–21; 2 Ch 16:1–6).

BABEL, TOWER OF Popular expression to describe the structure built on the plain of Shinar: Babel is the old name for **Babylon** (Ge 11:1–9).

BABYLON See page 42.

BALAAM A prophet bribed by **Balak** to curse the Israelites: instead he pronounced blessings (Nu 22–24).

BALAK King of Moab who hired **Balaam** to put a curse on Israel (Nu 22–24). Notorious as an example of the folly of trying to obstruct God's will (Jos 24:9; Jdg 11:25; Mic 6:5; Rev 2:14).

BAPTISM Being ceremonially washed in water to signify a new start in life. Submission to **John's** baptism was an expression of repentance (Mk 1:4; Ac 13:24) and a preparation for the ministry of Jesus, who would baptise not only with water but also with the **Holy Spirit** and fire (Mt 3:11). Jesus was baptised by John in order to identify with sinful humanity (Mt 3:13–17). After his **resurrection** Jesus sent his disciples into the world to preach, make converts and baptise them (Mt 28:19; Ac 2:41).

BARABBAS A Jewish revolutionary arrested by the Romans for murder (Mt 27:16; Mk 15:7). The priests prevailed upon **Pilate** to release him in substitution for Jesus (Mt 27:17, 20; Lk 23:18).

BARAK (lightning). Summoned by the prophetess **Deborah** to rally the Israelites against the Canaanite general, Sisera (Jdg 4–5). Hero of faith (Heb 11:32).

BARNABAS (encourager). Cousin of John **Mark** and member of Jewish-Cypriot family (Col 4:10). Important Christian leader who befriended **Saul** of Tarsus (Ac 9:27), represented the Jerusalem church in Antioch (Ac 11:26), engaged with Paul in a mission to Gentiles (Ac 13–14), and attended the council of Jerusalem (Ac 15). Later he parted from Paul (Ac 15:36–39).

BARTHOLOMEW (son of Ptolomy). Chosen by Jesus as one of the twelve apostles (Mt 10:3; Mk 3:18; Lk 6:14; Ac 1:13).

BARUCH (blessed). The devoted secretary of **Jeremiah** (Jer 36) who was exiled with him to Egypt (Jer 43:6).

BASHAN The broad, fertile area east of the Sea of **Galilee** (Nu 21:33–35; Dt 3:1–7; Ps 22:12; Isa 2:13; Eze 27:6).

BATHSHEBA Daughter of Eliam (2 Sa 11:3) and wife of Uriah. **David** plotted Uriah's death in order to marry her himself; he earned the rebuke of **Nathan**, the prophet (2 Sa 12). In David's old age she co-operated with Nathan to secure the succession of her son, Solomon (1 Ki 1).

BEATITUDES Sayings introduced by 'Blessed (happy) are . . .' (e.g. Mt 5:3–12; Lk 6:20–23).

BEELZEBUB NT version of Baal-Zebub, god of Ekron (2 Ki 1:2, 3, 6; Mt 10:25; 12:24; 12:27; Lk 11:15–19). See **Baal**. Identified with **Satan**.

BEERSHEBA (well of seven). A place, famous for its wells, 50 miles SW of Jerusalem. Here **Abraham** (Ge 21:31; 22:19), **Isaac** (Ge 26:33) and **Jacob** (Ge 28:10) settled. The most southerly place in the land of Israel as Dan was the most northerly (Jdg 20:1; 1 Sa 3:20; 2 Ch 30:5).

BELIEVERS Title given to those who believe that Jesus is the Christ and reigns as Lord in heaven (Ac 1:15; 2:44; Gal 6:10; 1 Pe 2:17).

BELSHAZZAR (may Bel protect the king). The last king of **Babylon** killed during its capture in 539 B.C. by Darius the Mede (Da 5).

BELTESHAZZAR (may Bel protect him). The name given to **Daniel** when exiled to Babylon (Da 1:7; 10:1).

BENEDICTUS (blessed). Latin title given to the prophecy of **Zechariah** (Lk 1:68–79), relating to **John the Baptist** and **Jesus**.

BENJAMIN (son of the right hand). **Benjamites**. **Jacob**'s youngest son, whose mother, **Rachel**, died at his birth (Ge 35:18, 24). After **Joseph** disappeared, he became his father's favourite son (Ge 42:4) and this relationship brought about the reconciliation of Joseph and his brothers (Ge 44). Benjamites were his descendants and as a tribe were famous for courage and fighting skills, with left-handed slingers (1 Ch 8; Jdg 3:15; 20:46; 1 Sa 9:1).

BETHANY (house of unripe figs). (1) Village two miles from **Jerusalem** on the **Jericho** road, the home of **Mary**, **Martha** and **Lazarus** (Jn 11:1) and of **Simon** the leper

(Mt 26:6). Here Jesus was anointed and he made it his base in his last week (Mt 21:17). (2) An unidentified place east of Jordan where John baptised (Jn 1:28).

BETHEL (house of God). Originally called Luz (Ge 28:19), some twelve miles north of **Jerusalem**. An ancient centre of worship (Ge 12:8; 1 Sa 7:16; 10:3) chosen by **Jeroboam I** to rival Jerusalem (1 Ki 12:26–29). Later denounced as a place of false worship (Am 3:14; Hos 10:15).

BETHLEHEM (house of bread). Town 5 miles SW of Jerusalem in the hill country of Judea. Originally called Ephrath and the site of the tomb of **Rachel** (Ge 35:19; 48:7). Home of **Boaz** (Ru 2:4) and **David** (1 Sa 16) and the place where the **Messiah** was to be born (Mic 5:2; Lk 2:4; Jn 7:42). Also the name of a place NW of **Nazareth** (Jos 19:15).

BETHPHAGE (house of figs). Village on the Mount of Olives, near **Bethany**, from where disciples borrowed an ass for Jesus (Mt 21:1; Mk 11:1; Lk 19:29).

BETHSAIDA (fisherman's house). Town on the north shore of the Sea of **Galilee** where Jesus went after feeding the 5,000 (Mk 6:45; Lk 9:10). The home of **Philip**, **Andrew** and **Peter** (Jn 1:44; 12:21).

BEZALEL (in God's shadow). A craftsman of Judah skilled in working wood, metal and precious stones; put in charge of constructing the **Tabernacle** (Ex 31; 35:30; 36:1; 37:1; 38:22; 2 Ch 1:5).

BILDAD One of the three friends of **Job**, whose speeches occur in Job 8; 18; 25. A traditional moralist, he divided men into the blameless or secretly wicked. God will prosper the one and destroy the other.

BILHAH Maidservant of **Rachel**, wife of **Jacob**, given to him to bear children. She bore **Dan** and **Naphtali** (Ge 29:29; 30:1–8).

BIRTHRIGHT. The firstborn son's privilege of succeeding his father as head of the family (Ge 25:31) with a double share of the property (Dt 21:17) to cover the extra duties involved.

BLASPHEMY Slander of God's honour, including contempt of sacred places (Ac 6:13), profane use of the divine name (Dt 5:11; Isa 52:5; Eze 36:20) and **idolatrous** worship (Eze 20:27). Punished by death (Lev 24:16; 1 Ki 21:13; Ac 7:58).

BLASPHEMY AGAINST THE HOLY SPIRIT Ascribing the actions of Jesus as God's **Messiah** to the **devil** (Mt 12:31; Mk 3:29; Lk 12:10).

BLESS, BLESSING God blesses (bestows good upon) nature (Ge 1:22), mankind (1:28), the **Sabbath** (2:3), nations (Ps 33:12) and individuals (Ge 24:1). Godly people respond by blessing (= adoring, worshipping, praising) God (Ps 103:1–2), and in word and action blessing (= bestowing good) on their fellows (Mt 5:44; 1 Pe 3:9).

BLINDNESS A common ailment in ancient times, sometimes interpreted as a divine punishment (Dt 28:28; Jn 9:2). Its healing was a feature of the arrival of the **Messiah** (Mt 11:5; Lk 4:18). Used metaphorically to describe lack of spiritual understanding (Mt 23:16; Jn 9:41; 2 Pe 1:9) and Satan's work (2 Co 4:4).

BLOOD The blood of animals was seen as being their life, created by God (Lev 17:11). However, with reference to animal sacrifices, the blood usually pointed to the violent death of the victim (Lev 1:5ff). **Atonement** for **sin** and pollution was gained by this sacrificial blood, poured out in **sacrifice** (Lev 17:11; Heb 9–10). In the NT the 'blood of Christ' means the sacrificial death of Jesus by which we are reconciled to God (Eph 1:7; 2:13; Col 1:20). The poured wine at the Last Supper pointed to the shed blood of Jesus (Mk 14:24; 1 Cor 11:25).

BOAZ A prosperous Bethlehem farmer who took the widow **Ruth** as his wife and became the great-grandfather of King **David** (Ru 2–4; Mt 1:5).

BODY Used metaphorically of the company of **believers** (Ro 12:4–5) and of the local and universal church of which Christ is the head and life-giver (Eph 4:12; 5:23; Col 1:18; 1 Co 12:27).

BOOK In ancient times a roll or scroll made of papyrus, leather or parchment (Jer 36; Rev 5:1, 5; 22:10). Books of the OT were usually written on separate scrolls, unless they were very brief (e.g. the Twelve Minor Prophets were put together). Many of the books referred to in the OT are now lost (Jos 10:13; 1 Ki 11:41).

BOOTH Temporary shelter made of boughs (Ne 8:15), used by soldiers in the field (1 Ki 20:12), as protection from the sun (Ge 33:17; Jnh 4:5) and in the **Feast of Tabernacles** as a reminder of Israel's nomadic life (Lev 23:34; Dt 16:13).

BREAD The main foodstuff in Israel made from barley, sometimes from wheat or spelt, normally with leaven on a griddle (Lev 23) or in a clay oven (Hos 7:4). Never cut, but broken by hand. The word is used of food in general and of material things in life (Dt 8:3; Mt 4:4). **Unleavened** bread was used when in a rush (Ge 19:3; Ru 2:14) and in remembrance of the hasty exodus from Egypt (Ex 12). Jesus spoke of himself as the bread of life (Jn 6:35).

BREATH The vital element in earthly life (Ge 1:30) given by God (Ge 2:7; Eze 37) and returned to him at death. Used of divine power (Job 4:9; 37:10; Ps 18:15) and of man's insignificance before God (Ps 62:9).

BRIDE Used metaphorically of the relationship of Israel to Yahweh (Jer 2:2) and of the church to Christ (Rev 21:2, 9).

BROTHERS OF THE LORD Half-brothers or stepbrothers or cousins of Jesus: they were **James**, Joseph,

Simon and **Jude** (Mt 13:55; Mk 6:3). They believed in Jesus as **Messiah** only after his resurrection (Jn 7:5; Ac 1:14; 1 Co 15:7).

BULL Calves used for sacrifice were usually one-year-old bulls (Lev 4:3ff; 9:2ff; 16:11ff). The Israelites were reprimanded for copying Egyptian bull-worship (Ex 32).

BURIAL Because of the climate burial was prompt, even for criminals (Dt 21:23). Family tombs (Jn 11:39), normally outside towns (Lk 7:12) were used (Ge 49:31). The corpse, wrapped in linen (Jn 11:44; 20:6) was carried on a bier accompanied by lamentation (Mk 5:38; Ac 8:2; Mt 9:23).

BURNING BUSH Scene of **Moses'** call to deliver Israel from the bondage of Egypt (Ex 3:3): the fire signified the divine presence (Jdg 13:20).

BURNT-OFFERING A sacrifice wholly burnt, except for the skin (Lev 7:8) to atone for sins (Lev 1:4). The victim had to be a clean animal (Ge 8:20) and without blemish (Lev 1:3). Sacrifices were made daily in the Temple (Nu 28–29).

CAESAR Title of Roman emperors. Augustus, 27 B.C.– A.D. 14 (Lk 2:1); Tiberius A.D. 14–37 (all other references in the four Gospels), Claudius A.D. 41–54 (Ac 11:28; 17:7; 18:2) and Nero (Php 4:22).

CAESAREA Mediterranean port, 23 miles south of Mount Carmel, built by **Herod** the Great in honour of Caesar Augustus. **Philip**, the evangelist (Ac 8:40) and the centurion Cornelius (Ac 10:1, 24) lived here.

CAESAREA PHILIPPI City, earlier called Paneas, below Mount Hermon, beautified by **Herod** the Great and **Philip** the tetrarch (who renamed it in honour of Augustus Caesar). The scene of Peter's confession of Christ (Mt 16:13; Mk 8:27).

CAIAPHAS High priest in Jerusalem (A.D. 18–36), son-in-law to Annas (Jn 18:13) his predecessor. In office at the time of Jesus' trial (Jn 11:49) and early persecution of Christians (Ac 4:6).

CAIN Eldest son of **Adam** and **Eve** (Ge 4), an agriculturalist who murdered his shepherd brother, **Abel**, out of jealousy and was exiled to the land of Nod (Heb 11:4; 1 Jn 3:12; Jude 11).

CALEB A courageous and loyal colleague of **Joshua** (Nu 14:6, 24) who was an outstanding commander in the invasion of Canaan (Jos 15:14).

CALENDAR Though an agricultural people, the Israelites used a lunar calendar whose year began in our March/April. The twelve months were: Nisan, Iyyar, Sivan, Tammuz, Ab, Elul, Tishri, Marchesvan, Chislev, Tebeth, Shebat and Adar (Est 2:16; 3:7; 8:9; Lev 23:5; Ne 2:1; 6:15).

CALF/CALVES, GOLDEN (1) The idol in the form of a golden calf made by **Aaron** and the Israelites and destroyed by Moses on his return from Mount Sinai (Ex 32). (2) The two idols in the form of golden calves set up by **Jeroboam I** of Israel at Bethel and Dan in order to divert worship away from Jerusalem in the neighbouring kingdom of **Judah** (1 Ki 12:28). Jehu's reforms did not remove them (2 Ki 10:29) and **Hosea** (8:6) spoke of their destruction.

CALVARY The Latinised version of Golgotha (Aramaic) meaning 'skull' (Mt 27:33); the place of Jesus' crucifixion. See **Skull**.

CANA (place of reeds). A village 9 miles north of Nazareth where Jesus turned water into wine (Jn 2:1) and healed the son of a nobleman (Jn 4:46).

CANAAN (1) Son of Ham (Ge 9:18) and grandson of **Noah** who laid a curse on him (Ge 9:25). His descendants are listed in Ge 10:15–19. (2) A Semitic-speaking people and their homeland (strictly the south Palestine coast (Nu 13:29; Dt 1:7); however, the term was applied to Palestine in general (Ge 12:5; Nu 13:17).

CANAANITE (merchant). See page 41.

CAPERNAUM (Nahum's village). Town by the Sea of **Galilee** and frontier post of the tetrarchies of **Herod** and **Philip** (Mt 17:24), a Roman military base (Mt 8:5) and home of **Peter** and **Andrew** (Mk 1:29). Jesus made it his headquarters (Mt 4:13) but people there were unresponsive to him (Lk 4:23; 10:15).

CARMEL (fruitful). A range of hills stretching for 70 miles from the bay of Acre to Dothan and having dense vegetation (Am 1:2; 9:3; Na 1:4). The prophet **Elijah** challenged the gods of **Jezebel** here (1 Ki 18:19ff).

CENTURION Roman officer in charge of 60–100 men. Several had favourable encounters with Jesus and the Church (Mt 8:5; 27:54; Lk 7:2; 23:47; Ac 10:1; 27:43).

CEPHAS (rock). Corresponds to the Greek, **Peter**, the name given to the apostle **Simon** by Jesus (Jn 1:42; 1 Co 1:12; 3:22).

CHALDEA/CHALDEANS Chaldea is the alternative name for **Babylonia** (Eze 23:15–16; Ezr 5:12), the modern Southern Iraq.

CHERUBIM Spiritual beings who guarded the tree of life in Eden (Ge 3:24). Golden representations with outstretched wings were set on the lid (= mercy seat) of the **Ark** of the covenant (Ex 25:18; Heb 9:5). In Ezekiel's vision the cherubim carry the chariot-throne of God (Eze 10). Large cherubim carved in olive wood and overlaid with gold decorated Solomon's Temple (1 Ki 6:23–28).

CHRIST Greek form of Hebrew **Messiah** meaning 'the anointed one'. See **Jesus Christ**.

CHRISTIAN Used for the first time at Antioch of a follower of Jesus Christ (Ac 11:26; 26:28; 1 Pe 4:16). Also called Nazarenes (Ac 24:5), brother (Ac 9:17), **disciple** (Ac 9:36) and **believer** (Ac 10:45).

CHURCH In the NT not a building but a local congregation of Christians (Ac 15:4) or the whole body of Christians (Eph 5:23). Entry is by **confession** of Christ (Mt 16:18) and **baptism** (Ac 2:41).

CILICIA Part of south-east Asia Minor (Ac 6:9; 15:23, 41; 27:5; Gal 1:21). Tarsus, Paul's home town, was the leading city (Ac 21:39; 22:3; 23:34).

CIRCUMCISION The ancient custom of cutting off the male foreskin (usually soon after birth) practised in many places in the ancient Near East, including Israel (Ge 17:10). It symbolised for the latter **covenant** membership of God's people and was normally carried out on the eighth day after birth (Lev 12:3). To be circumcised meant that one was loyal to God (Dt 10:16; Jer 9:25; Ro 2:29). The church in the NT refused to impose circumcision upon non-Jews who were baptised (Ac 15; Ro 3:30; 1 Co 7:19; Gal 5:2, 6; 6:15; Php 3:3; Col 2:11).

CITIES OF REFUGE Places where anyone responsible of accidental manslaughter could flee for refuge (Nu 35; Dt 19; Jos 20). The purpose was to prevent inter-family blood feuds escalating.

CITY OF GOD Jerusalem is both the holy city (Mt 5:35) and the sinful city which kills the **prophets** (Mt 23:37). The true city of God is being created in **heaven** and will descend to earth as the centre of the new age of the kingdom of God (Heb 12:22–23, 40; Rev 21–22; Gal 4:24–26).

CLAUDIUS Roman emperor A.D. 41–54 who banished Jews from Rome in A.D. 49 (Ac 18:2).

CLEAN In the OT there is a division between clean and unclean which is fundamental to Israelite religion. The **LORD** is to be served by physically clean people (Ex 19:10ff; 30:18ff), who are ritually and ceremonially clean (Lev 14:1ff; 15:1ff), and who are morally clean of heart (Ps 51:7). In the NT the emphasis is virtually wholly on the clean/pure heart (Mk 7:1–23; Mt 5:8). See **unclean**.

CLOUD, PILLAR OF A luminous cloud, symbol of the presence and glory of God, which guided the Israelites in the wilderness (Ex 13:21–22). At night it became a fire. It rested on the movable **sanctuary** (Ex 29:42–3; 40:34–8). In the NT it is associated with the **transfiguration** (Mt 17:5), **Ascension** (Ac 1:9) and second advent (Rev 1:7) of Jesus.

COLOSSE An ancient city of Phrygia in western Asia Minor on the south bank of the Lycus river. It stood on the trade route from Ephesus to the Euphrates. The church here was established by Epaphras (Col 1:7, 12–13) but **Paul** wrote a letter to it, now in the NT. The Turks destroyed the city in the twelfth century.

COMMANDMENTS, TEN A code of **law** which summarises the essence of the Law of Moses. Found in Ex 20, and Dt 5 and accepted by Jesus. He further reduced the ten to two commandments—to love God and one's neighbour (Mt 22:34–40).

COMPASSION Mercy and pity shown both by God to human beings (Ex 33:10; Ps 51:1; 90:13; Isa 14:1; 54:8; Mt 20:34; 2 Co 1:3) and by human beings to one another (Col 3:12; Eph 4:32).

CONCUBINE A woman living with a man not her husband: it was common among the early Israelites. The households of **Abraham** (Ge 16:2) and **Jacob** (Ge 29:24) provide examples: the law of Moses protected her (Ex 21:7–11; Dt 21:10–14). She was distinguished from a wife (2 Sa 5:13; 1 Ki 11:3). Not regarded as immoral and the children of a concubine were accepted as legitimate.

CONFESSION To acknowledge **sin** before God (Lev 5:5; Ne 1:6; 1 Jn 1:9) and also to state publicly an allegiance to God/Christ (Ro 10:9; Php 2:11). Both aspects are central to the genuine **faith** in both OT and NT.

CONSCIENCE The moral sense of right and wrong, present to some degree in all human beings (Ro 1:19). A bad conscience can be cleansed (Heb 10:22) and all consciences need enlightening by God (Heb 9:14) since to defy the promptings of conscience can wreck **faith** (1 Ti 1:19). A Christian is to have a good or clear conscience (Ro 9:1; 1 Co 4:4; 1 Ti 1:5).

CONSECRATE To set aside for God and his service (Ex 13:2; 28:3, 38).

CORINTH Busy commercial city on the central isthmus of Greece and capital of the Roman province of Achaia. **Paul** stayed here for 18 months in A.D. 52 (Ac 18). Two thirds of the population were slaves and its immorality was proverbial. Two letters from Paul to the church he founded are in the NT.

CORNELIUS A Roman **centurion** of the cohort stationed at **Caesarea**, a 'God-fearer', who became the first Gentile convert to Christ (Ac 10).

COUNCIL See **Sanhedrin**.

COUNCIL OF JERUSALEM The assembly held in A.D. 48 of representatives from the church in Antioch, led by **Paul** and **Barnabas**, and the leaders of the church in Jerusalem, to discuss the influx of Gentiles into the Church (Ac 15).

COUNSELLOR Name given to the Messiah (Isa 9:6) and to the Holy Spirit (Jn 14:16, 26; 15:26; 16:7). The original Greek word is 'paracletos' and means 'one called alongside to help'.

COVENANT An agreement made to regulate relationships between two unequal parties, involving obligations and promises. God made covenants with **Noah** (Ge 6:18), the **patriarchs** (Ge 15:18; Ro 11:27), **Israel** (Ex 24) and **David** (2 Sa 7). The covenant was sealed with the blood of sacrifice (Ex 24:8; Zec 9:11). The inability of the people to keep the covenant (Heb 8:7) was foreseen by **Jeremiah** who spoke of a future, new covenant written in the heart (Jer 31:31). This **prophecy** was fulfilled in the covenant inaugurated by the sacrificial **blood** of Jesus (Mt 26:28; Lk 22:20; 1 Co 11:25).

CREATION God as **LORD** is presented as Creator (Ge 1:1; Rev 4:11) as also is the eternal Son of God (Jn 1:14; 1 Co 8:6; Col 1:16; Heb 1:2). A poetic account of the order of creation is given in Ge 1–2. However, since the 'old' creation is infected with evil and sin, God is making a new creation in which Jesus is the new **Adam**, the head of a **redeemed** humanity (1 Co 15:22, 45; Eph 1:22) which will live in a new **heaven** and earth (Rev 21–22).

CREED A statement of belief. The **Apostles'** Creed belongs to a later period than the NT. All we find in the NT are short summaries of faith—e.g. Ro 1:3; 8:34; Php 2:5–11; 2 Ti 2:8; 1 Ti 3:16. The classic OT creed is in Dt 6:4ff and is called the 'shema'.

CRETE An island 60 miles south of Greece where Paul's ship to Rome called (Ac 27:8). Titus was instructed by Paul to evangelise there (Tit 1:5). In OT times the home of the Kerethites (2 Sa 15:18).

CROSS Stake on which a condemned man was tied or impaled by the Romans. Three types were used—shaped like a capital T or X or like a plus sign +. The description of Jesus' cross as a tree (Ac 5:30; 10:39; 13:29) alludes to the curse attached to a dead body hung on a tree (Dt 21:22–23; Gal 3:13). 'Taking his cross' was used by Jesus to refer to the possible suffering of his **disciples** (Mt 10:38). Jesus himself suffered and died on a cross at **Golgotha** (Mt 27:32ff).

CRUCIFIXION Roman form of capital punishment taken over from the Phoenicians and Carthaginians by the Romans. Used for slaves and the worst of criminals but rarely for Roman citizens. The victim was scourged (Mt 27:26) then made to carry the cross or beam to the place of execution (Jn 19:17). Doped and then nailed by hands and feet he was left hanging just above ground level until he died.

CUBIT A linear measurement, equivalent to the distance from elbow to finger-tip, about 17½ inches, and much used in OT times (Ex 25:10, 17). The longer or royal cubit was a hand's breadth more, about 20½ inches (Eze 40:5).

CURSE Not using profane language but the reverse of 'to bless'. At the human level to wish harm or catastrophe (Nu 23:7; Job 31:30; Rom 12:14; Jas 3:9). When God utters a curse it is either a denunciation of sin (Nu 5:21, 23; Dt 29:19–20) or his actual judgment upon sin (Nu 5:22, 24, 27; Isa 24:6). There is an intimate relationship between obedience and blessing, disobedience and cursing in the **covenant** (Dt 11:26–28; Isa 1:19–20); thus the law itself is a curse to those who fail to obey it (Gal 3:10, 13).

CYPRUS Island in the eastern Mediterranean (OT Elishah, Eze 27:7), home of **Barnabas** (Ac 4:36) and Mnason (Ac 21:16). **Paul** and Barnabas preached here (Ac 13) and Barnabas later returned with **Mark** (Ac 15:39).

CYRUS II (THE GREAT) Persian king (559–530 B.C.) who conquered **Babylon** in 539 B.C. He allowed exiled Jews to return to Judah (2 Ch 36:22; Ezr 1:1) and restore the Temple (Ezr 6:3). Daniel was in his service (Da 6:28; 10:1).

DAGON Chief god of the Philistines worshipped at Gaza (Jdg 16:23), Ashdod (1 Sa 5:5) and Beth Shan (1 Sa 31:10 & 1 Ch 10:10).

DAMARIS An Athenian woman of high social rank converted to Christ by **Paul** at Athens (Ac 17:34).

DAMASCUS Capital of Syria (Isa 7:8) or Aram (1 Ki 11:24) and set astride trading routes (1 Ki 20:34) linking Egypt and Arabia with the East. It has been continuously occupied from pre-historic times. Captured by **David** (2 Sa 8:5; 1 Ch 18:5) it later gained independence under Ben-Hadad (1 Ki 15:18). **Saul** of Tarsus was converted to Christ here (Ac 9).

DAN Son of Jacob and Bilhah (Ge 30:6) and ancestor of the tribe of Dan. The latter was one of the twelve tribes of Israel (Ge 14:14), settling first west of the **Dead Sea** (Jos 19:40) but later, under Amorite pressure (Jdg 1:34) some members migrated northwards to the neighbourhood of Tyre (Jos 19:47). These northern Danites were deported to Assyria in 732 B.C. (2 Ki 15:29). The tribe is strangely omitted from the list in Rev 7.

Dan is also the name of the most northerly Israelite settlement, earlier called Laish or Leshem (Jdg 18:29; Jos 19:47). See **Beersheba**.

DANIEL (God is my judge). The name of four men. (1) Second son of **David** and Abigail (1 Ch 3:1). (2) Exiled priest, descendant of Ithamar who returned from Babylon with Ezra (Ezr 8:2; Ne 10:6). (3) A man outstanding for his godly wisdom, classed with Noah and Job (Eze 14:14,20; 28:3). (4) The fourth of the major prophets, a young Jew of noble descent deported to Babylon in 597 B.C. He was renamed Belteshazzar and employed by Nebuchadnezzar

(Da 1) and other kings. His prophecies constitute the book of Daniel which Jesus quoted (Mt 24:15).

DARIUS A common name for Medo-Persian rulers. (1) Darius the Mede (= **Cyrus II**) became king of the Chaldeans in 559 B.C. (Da 5:30–31). (2) Darius I (521–486 B.C.) king of Persia and Babylon, who authorised exiled Jews to return to Jerusalem and rebuild the Temple (Ezr 4:5; Hag 1:1; Zec 1:1). (3) Darius II (423–408 B.C.) called Darius the Persian in Ne 12:22. His kingdom was destroyed by Alexander the Great.

DARKNESS Used in both OT and NT in a literal and figurative sense. The latter includes darkness as the sphere of **evil** (Lk 22:53), **Satan** (Ac 26:18; Rev 16:10), the destiny of the wicked (1 Sa 2:9; Mt 8:12) and of the enemies of God (Na 1:8). Christ is said to bring **light** to those in darkness (Jn 1:5; 1 Jn 2:8).

DAVID Youngest of Jesse's eight sons and second king of Israel (1 Sa 16–1 Ki 2; 1 Ch 2–29). He overcame Israel's enemies and prepared for the building of the Temple in Jerusalem (1 Ch 22). He was skilled in music (1 Sa 18:10; Am 6:5) in composing elegies (2 Sa 1:19) and psalms (2 Sa 23:1), 78 of which are ascribed to him in the book of Psalms. Ancestor of Jesus (Mt 1:17) and prophet of the coming of the **Messiah** and of his resurrection (Ac 1:16; 2:31). 'Son of David' was a title for the Messiah (Mt 12:23; Lk 20:41).

DAY OF THE LORD The final day of the present age when God will judge Israel and all the nations (Am 5:18–20; Isa 2:12f; Zep 1:7). In the NT this day is further explained as the day of the second coming of Christ to earth as the King and Judge (2 Th 2:2; 1 Co 1:8; 5:5; 2 Pe 3:12ff).

DEACON A semi-technical word for those who had particular duties of service (caring for sick and poor) in the early churches (Php 1:1; 1 Ti 3:8–13). Phoebe is called a servant/deaconess of the Church in Ro 16:1; she probably assisted at baptisms of women.

DEAD SEA An inland lake, 47 miles long and 3–9 miles wide, fed by the **Jordan**. At 1,293 feet below sea level it is the lowest body of water in the world. It loses water only by evaporation, making it five times saltier than the sea. This name only occurs from the second century A.D.: before then called the Salt Sea (Ge 14:3), Eastern Sea (Eze 47:18) and Sea of the Arabah (Dt 4:49). In one vision **Ezekiel** saw a river of pure water flowing from Jerusalem to bring life to this sea (Eze 47:8–12).

DEATH Both the OT and NT present death as belonging to human sinful existence and the result not merely of biological forces but of the effects of **sin** (Ro 5:12). It is the return to the earth of the dust of which mankind is made (Ge 3:19); thus mortals ought to trust in the Lord to preserve them in and through death (Ps 73:23–34; 139:8). But there is also spiritual death, the lack of spiritual communion between God and a human being. This causes separation from God even after death (Rev 2:11; 20:6). Jesus Christ died in order to destroy the power of death (Heb 2:9, 14; Rev 1:8), to reconcile sinners to God (Ro 5:10), to bring them into communion with God and to gain for them the **resurrection** of the body (1 Co 15).

DEBORAH (bee) (1) The nurse of **Rebekah**. A tree marks the spot where she was buried at Bethel (Ge 35:8). (2) A prophetess/charismatic leader of the tribes of Israel. She ordered Barak to lead the Israelites against Sisera (Jdg 4–5). The victory song of Deborah (Jdg 5) is one of the oldest passages in the OT.

DEBT In the OT personal loans between Israelites were not supposed to be subject to interest. However, failure to pay and with no security to forfeit could result in debtors being sold into slavery (Ex 22:3; 2 Ki 4:1; Am 2:6; 8:6) for limited periods (Lev 25:39–55). The NT reflects a more complex economy and little regard for the old Mosaic law (Mt 25:16–27; Jn 2:13–17) and Jesus taught compassion towards those in debt (Mt 18:23–35). In the **Lord's Prayer** 'debts' conveys the idea of the guilt of unpaid moral obligations to God (Mt 6:12).

DECAPOLIS From 63 B.C. a federation of ten towns, S and E of the Sea of **Galilee**. Crowds from this area followed Jesus (Mt 4:25) who landed at one town, Gerasa (Mk 5:1) where the swine went headlong over the cliff. Much of the population was **Gentile** but Jesus revisited (Mk 7:31).

DEDICATION, FEAST OF An eight-day festival originally to celebrate the winter solstice (Jn 10:22) but later to commemorate the reconsecration of the **Temple** by Judas Maccabeus in 164 B.C., three years after its defilement by Antiochus Epiphanes. Also called the Feast of Lights from the special illumination in homes for the festival (Jn 9:5).

DEFILEMENT See **unclean**.

DELILAH (delicate). Philistine woman who ensnared Samson (Jdg 16).

DEMAS Colleague of **Paul** (Col 4:14; Phm 24) who later, out of self interest, deserted the imprisoned apostle (2 Ti 4:10).

DEMETRIUS (1) A silversmith at Ephesus who instigated a riot against Paul because the apostle's preaching was shrinking the trade in silver shrines, made to honour the god **Artemis** (Diana)—Ac 19:24, 28. (2) A disciple with an outstanding Christian witness (3 Jn 12).

DEMON In the four gospels there are many references to spiritual (invisible) beings who are hostile to God and to human beings. Their prince is **Satan** (Mk 3:22) and they are deemed responsible for a variety of human illnesses as well as what we call demon-possession (Lk 11:14; Mk 9:17ff). Jesus was in continual conflict with them (Lk 10:17– 20). Paul taught that **idolatry** was demonic (1 Co 10:19ff; Dt 32:17).

DERBE A city, 100 miles NW of Tarsus, in Lycaonia (Asia Minor) visited by **Paul** and **Barnabas** when founding the churches of south Galatia (Ac 14:6, 20; 16:1). Home of Gaius (Ac 20:4).

DESCENT INTO HADES/HELL An expression used in the Apostles' Creed and based on 1 Pe 3:19; 4:6. Between his physical death and bodily **resurrection** the spirit of Jesus was alive, proclaiming his victory to the realm of the dead.

DESOLATION For 'the abomination that causes desolation' (Mt 24:15; Mk 13:14) recalling Da 9:27; 11:31; 12:11, see **abomination**.

DEVIL (slanderer). One of the principal titles of **Satan**, the arch-enemy of God and of human beings (Rev 12:9). He attacks individuals (Mt 13:39; Lk 8:12; Rev 2:10) and has the power of death (Heb 2:14). The Christian must resist him (Eph 6:11) for in the end he will be destroyed (Heb 2:14; Rev 20:10). See **Satan**.

DISCIPLE (a learner). A pupil of some teacher: thus disciples of **John the Baptist** (Mt 9:14), the **Pharisees** (Mt 22:16) or, of Jesus (Mt 5:1; 8:21, 23, 25). Those who were called apostles were also disciples (Mt 10:1). Learning was both by listening and watching (imitating)—Mt 11:29. See **believers**.

DISCIPLE, BELOVED An un-named apostle (probably John) mentioned in the fourth gospel (Jn 19:26; 20:2; 21:7).

DISEASE See **health and disease**.

DISPERSION The term **diaspora** (= dispersion) can denote either Jews living away from Palestine in non-Jewish countries (Jn 7:35; 1 Pe 1:1) or the actual towns where they lived (Jas 1:1). Such Jews sought to attend Jerusalem at the time of a festival (Ac 2:5–12).

DIVINATION The pseudo-science of predicting future events by means of the occult. It was strictly forbidden in Israel (Lev 19:31; 20:6; Dt 18:10–11), was condemned by prophets (Isa 2:6; 8:19) and one of the sins which led to the fall of the kingdom of Israel (2 Ki 17:17).

DIVORCE Under the law of Moses a husband could divorce his wife under certain conditions (Dt 22:13–19, 28–29; 24:1–4; Hos 2:4). Jesus taught that he who divorces his wife and marries another commits **adultery** and she who is divorced and marries another commits adultery (Mk 10:1–12; Lk 16:18). **Paul** taught a similar doctrine (1 Co 7:10–11). There is discussion as to what the phrase 'except for unlawful sexual intercourse' in Mt 5:32 means. The NIV translates it as 'marital unfaithfulness' and so presents Jesus as allowing divorce for this reason.

DOVE Member of the pigeon family, a **clean** bird and therefore acceptable both for food and sacrifice (Lev 12:6, 8; 14:22; Lk 2:24). Chosen by **Noah** as the first bird to find out when the flood waters had gone down (Ge 8:8). Figuratively, it describes the descent of the **Holy Spirit** upon Jesus at his baptism (Mt 3:16) and the virtue of innocence (Mt 10:16).

DRAGON Used figuratively of **Satan** in Rev 12–13; 16:13; 20:2.

DREAM In the Bible there are records of ordinary dreams (Ge 40:9–17; 41:1–7) which relate to things/events in ordinary life. Then there are dreams which actually communicate a message from God (1 Ki 3:5–15; Mt 1:20–24; Ac 16:9ff). For Israelites there was a close relation between dream and **prophecy** (Dt 13:1–5; Jer 23:25–32; Nu 12:6–8). Matthew's gospel records five dreams concerning the birth/infancy of Jesus (1:20; 2:12–13, 19, 22).

DRINK OFFERING Offered to God along with the cereal gift (Ex 29:38–42; Lev 23:13) as an acknowledgment that

he is the provider of basic food and drink. It was of wine
which was poured over the **altar**.

DUST Though used literally (2 Sa 15:32; 1 Ki 20:10) it is
often used figuratively of a multitude (Ge 13:16; Isa 29:5),
smallness (Dt 9:21; 2 Ki 13:7), poverty (1 Sa 2:8), abase-
ment (Ge 18:27; Job 42:6) and death (Ps 22:15). Dust on
the head was a sign of distress (Job 2:12; Rev 18:19) or
contrition (Jos 7:6). It also signified man's lowly origin (Ge
2:7; 1 Co 15:47).

EARTHQUAKE Earthquakes were reasonably common in
the ancient Near East; several are recorded in the Bible
—Ex 19:18; 1 Sa 14:15; Nu 16:31; 1 Ki 19:11; Am 1:1; Zec
14:5; Mt 28:2; Ac 16:26. Before the end of the age earthquakes will become more common (Mt 24:7; Rev 6:12;
11:13; 16:18). An earthquake was seen as descriptive of
divine judgment (Isa 29:6; Eze 38:19ff).

EBAL, MOUNT The northern and higher of the two
mountains overshadowing Shechem; the other was **Gerizim**. **Moses** commanded that the curses of the law be recited
by six tribes from Ebal (Dt 5–11; 27:9–28:68; Jos 8:30–35).

EBENEZER (stone of help). (1) A place where the **Philistines** overwhelmed Israel and the **Ark** of the Covenant was
captured (1 Sa 4:1; 5:1). (2) The name given to a stone put
up by **Samuel** to mark his victory over the Philistines,
thus reversing the earlier defeat (1 Sa 7:12).

EDEN, GARDEN OF The place where **Adam** and **Eve** lived
from the time of their creation (Ge 2:8) and from which
they were expelled (Ge 3:23). Its beauty was proverbial
(Eze 31:18; 36:35; Joel 2:3). Also called the 'garden of
God' (Eze 28:13; 31:8–9) and of the Lord (Isa 51:3).

EDOM (red). (1) Firstborn son of **Isaac** and twin brother of
Jacob; named Esau at birth but called Edom after selling
his birthright (Ge 25:30). (2) The descendants of Edom

(Ge 36:1–17; Nu 20:18, 20–21; Am 1:6, 11; Mal 1:4).
(3) The land occupied by the Edomites, formerly the land
of Seir (Ge 32:3; 36:20–21; Nu 24:18) situated between the
Dead Sea and the Gulf of Aqaba.

EDUCATION In traditional Israelite society a boy would
learn morality from his mother and his trade from his
father. A girl was taught wholly by her mother both morality and domestic duties. In the keeping of the **Sabbath** and
the **festivals** religion was learned and absorbed by all.
Education was based on the maxim: 'The fear of the LORD
is the beginning of knowledge' (Pr 1:7).

EGLON (1) King of **Moab**, remarkable for obesity, whose
assassination by **Ehud** led to Israel's deliverance from
bondage (Jdg 3:12–30). (2) City near Lachish occupied by
tribe of Judah (Jos 10:3–37; 12:12; 15:39).

EGYPT See page 41.

EHUD (1) A left-handed Benjamite, the second **judge** of
Israel, who assassinated **Eglon**, king of Moab (Jdg 3:15–
30). (2) Son of Bilhan, a Benjamite (1 Ch 7:10; 8:6).

EKRON One of the five fortified cities of the **Philistines**.
The **Ark** of the Covenant, captured by the Philistines, was
lodged here for a while (1 Sa 5:10).

ELAH (terebinth). The name of five men in the OT but
chiefly of the son of Baasha, king of Israel 886–885 B.C.
(1 Ki 16:6–14).

ELAM (highlands). (1) A mountainous region to the east
of Babylonia with its capital at Susa (Shushan). The all-
conquering Assyrians deported some Elamites to Samaria
and some Israelites to Elam (Ezr 4:9; Isa 11:11). Elamite
Jews were in Jerusalem for the feast of **Pentecost** (Ac 2:9).
(2) Elamites were descendants of Elam, a son of Shem (Ge
10:22; 1 Ch 1:17).

ELDAD AND MEDAD Two of the seventy elders of the tribes of Israel who received the gift of prophecy, even though they did not go with the other sixty-eight to the **Tabernacle** (Nu 11:24–29).

ELDER One in the community vested with authority on grounds of seniority in age or experience (Ex 3:16; Nu 22:4). The elders of Israel were influential locally (Ru 4:2) and nationally (1 Sa 8:4; 2 Sa 5:3). By NT times their civic authority had been extended to include religious power (Mt 15:2; 21:23; 26:3; Ac 4:5). The Christian Church made similar appointments, following the lead of the **synagogue** with its elders (Ac 14:23; 1 Ti 4:14; Tit 1:5; 1 Pe 5:1).

ELEAZAR (God has helped). Most OT occurrences of this common name refer to the third son of Aaron (Ex 6:23) who succeeded his father as high priest (Nu 20:25–28). From him were descended one of the two main divisions of the full priesthood ('sons of Aaron') and almost all the high priests down to the second century B.C.

ELECTION God's free choice of a family (tribe/nation) or an individual to enjoy his salvation and to serve him in a particular way. This is a prominent theme of the whole Bible since God elected the people of Israel (Dt 28:1–14; Isa 43:10–12, 20, 21) and from within Israel particular individuals—e.g. **David** (1 Sa 10:24). In the NT Jesus is the 'elect one' (Lk 9:35; 1 Pe 2:4–6) and in and with him God has chosen a people to enjoy his salvation and praise his name (Eph 1:5; 1 Co 1:27ff; Ro 9–11).

ELI High priest and predecessor of **Samuel** as **judge** in Israel (1 Sa 1–4).

ELIJAH (Yahweh is God). The outstanding ninth century prophet of Israel, a native of Tishbi in Gilead (1 Ki 17:1). He consistently opposed **Ahab** and **Ahaziah** for allowing the worship of **Baal** (1 Ki 17–21; 2 Ki 1–2). His dramatic removal to heaven in a whirlwind was observed by his successor, Elisha (2 Ki 2). His return to address Israel was prophesied (Mal 4:5–6), and this expectation was seen in the NT as fulfilled by the ministry of **John the Baptist** (Mt 17:10–12). Elijah appeared with **Moses** on the mountain when Jesus was transfigured (Mt 17:3).

ELIM (trees). A camp of the Israelites on their journey from Egypt to Canaan. It has twelve springs and seventy palm trees (Ex 15:27; Nu 33:9).

ELISHA (God is salvation). Successor of **Elijah**, a ninth century prophet of Israel (1 Ki 19:16–21) who ministered for fifty years through the reigns of **Ahab**, **Ahaziah**, **Jehoram**, **Jehu**, **Jehoahaz** and **Jehoash** (1 Ki 19; 2 Ki 2–9; 13). Jesus referred to him (Lk 4:27).

ELIZABETH (God has redeemed). Wife of the priest **Zechariah** and mother of **John the Baptist**; relative of **Mary**, mother of Jesus (Lk 1:5–57).

ELOI, ELOI, LAMA SABACHTHANI Jesus' cry of desolation from the **cross** (Mt 27:46). The words are in Aramaic and from Ps 22:1.

EMMANUEL See **Immanuel**.

EMMAUS A village 7 miles from **Jerusalem**, destination of Cleopas and another disciple of Jesus on Easter evening. As they walked, Jesus came to walk with them (Lk 24:13).

ENOCH (consecrated). (1) Eldest son of Cain after whom the first city was named (Ge 4:17–18). (2) Son of Jared (Ge 5:18) and father of Methuselah (Ge 5:21–22). He walked with God (Ge 5:24) and was taken to heaven without dying (Heb 11:5–6).

EPHESUS The major port in Roman Asia Minor (now 6 miles from the sea, due to silting of the river Cayster). It had a massive open-air theatre (Ac 19:29) and a famous temple to the goddess **Artemis** (Ac 19:27). **Paul** visited several times (Ac 19:1; 1 Co 16:8), and left **Timothy** in charge of the church there (1 Ti 1:3). **John** wrote a letter (Rev 2:1–7) to this church.

EPHOD (1) A garment something like an apron worn over the breast of the **high priest**, suspended from the shoulders by two straps and decorated with twelve precious stones (Ex 28:6–14; 39:2–7). It also had a pouch in which were kept **Urim and Thummim** (Ex 28:15–30; 39:8–21). (2) Some kind of image, whose shape is uncertain (Jdg 17:5; 18:14, 18, 20).

EPHRAIM (fruitful). (1) Second son of **Joseph** (Ge 41:50–52), who by the blessing of his grandfather, **Jacob**, became more important in Israel's history than his elder brother **Manasseh** (Ge 48). (2) Ephraim's descendants were allocated territory by **Joshua** which was called Ephraim (Jos 16).

EPICUREANS Philosophers who followed the teaching of Epicurus (341–270 B.C.). Paul came across them in Athens (Ac 17:18). They sought happiness through peaceful detachment from worldly pleasures.

ESARHADDON Son and successor of the Assyrian king, **Sennacherib** (2 Ki 19:37; Isa 37:38). Famous for rebuilding Babylon and military exploits. Reigned 681–669 B.C.

ESAU (hairy). The favourite of **Isaac**'s twin sons. Although the elder his inferiority to his brother, **Jacob**, was forecast at birth (Ge 25:23) and confirmed by Isaac's dying blessing (Ge 27:22–29). Ancestor of the **Edomites** (Ge 36:9).

ESTHER A Jewish orphan girl who became queen of Persia when she married Ahasuerus (= Xerxes, 486–465 B.C.). She was able to save her fellow-Jews from destruction. See the book of Esther in the OT.

ETERNAL LIFE The quality of life that belongs to God (Ro 2:7; 6:23; Tit 1:2; 1 Jn 5:11), which is his gift to those who believe and trust in the Lord Jesus Christ (Jn 3:15–16, 36; 10:28; 17:3). It continues through physical death into the age of the kingdom of God, which is to come.

ETHIOPIA (burnt face). Not the modern state, but part of the kingdom of Nubia stretching from present-day Khartoum to Aswan and often called Cush, after the original settlers (Ge 10:6; 1 Ch 1:8–10). They were the most southern people known to the Hebrews. **Moses** married an Ethiopian (Nu 12:1). Hebrew prophets speak of the ultimate ruin of the kingdom of Ethiopia because it sought to overcome **Judah** in the days of king **Hezekiah** (2 Ki 19:9; Isa 37:9; Eze 29:10; 30:4–5; 38:5; Zeph 3:10).

EUCHARIST See **Lord's Supper**.

EUNUCH A confidential court official (Est 2:3; 2 Ki 9:32) usually a castrate. The treasurer at the court of Candace of Ethiopia was a eunuch converted to Christ (Ac 8:26–40). Jesus used the word to refer to someone who renounces marriage in order to serve God more freely (Mt 19:12).

EUPHRATES The largest river in west Asia (the river of Dt 11:24) running 1,250 miles into the Persian Gulf. Often mentioned in the Bible (Ge 2:14; Ex 23:31; Dt 1:7; Jos 1:4; 2 Sa 8:3; 2 Ki 24:7; Isa 27:12; Jer 46:2, 6; Rev 9:14).

EVANGELIST Name given to the writers of the four Gospels. And a person whose primary task in life is to proclaim the good news concerning Jesus (Ac 21:8; Eph 4:11; 2 Ti 4:5).

EVE (life). The first woman; wife of **Adam**, mother of **Cain**, **Abel** and **Seth** (Ge 3:20; 4:1; 1 Ti 2:13). Used by **Satan** to tempt Adam to eat the forbidden fruit and so disobey God (2 Co 11:3).

EVIL There is a difference between physical evil (e.g. suffering) and moral evil (e.g. murder). God is presented as the Sovereign who tolerates evil in his universe, and even uses the existence of physical evil for good purposes (Ro 8:38–39 and the experience of Job). God is separate from all moral evil and is in no way responsible for it. He will finally banish it from the universe (Rev 21:1–8). Meanwhile God is involved in a conflict with evil power (Eph 6:10–17). **Satan**, the 'evil one', is committed to moral evil which may often be experienced as physical evil (Mt 5:37; 6:13; 13:19; 2 Th 3:3; 1 Jn 2:13–14).

EVIL SPIRITS A term used in Luke's writings to describe malignant powers (Lk 7:21; 8:2; 11:26; Ac 19:12). Another name for demons or unclean spirits under the control of **Satan**.

EXILE The leading members of the ten northern tribes (kingdom of Israel) were carried away captive by the Assyrians in 732 and 722 B.C. (2 Ki 15:29; 17:6). A century later Nebuchadnezzar deported to Babylon all but the poorest classes of Judah (2 Ki 24–25). When the Persians came to power seventy years later (Jer 25:11–12; 29:10; Da 9:2) exiled Jews were allowed to return (Ezra–Nehemiah tells the story). There is uncertainty as to what happened to the ten tribes of Israel in Assyria.

EXODUS The escape of the Israelite tribes, led by Moses, from servitude in Egypt. This event marked the birth of Israel as a nation (Ex 12), and it was constantly recalled as a great redemption caused by God himself (Jdg 6:8; 1 Sa 12:6; 1 Ki 8:51; 2 Ch 7:22; Ne 9:9; Ps 78:12; Isa 11:16; Jer 2:6; Eze 20:9; Ac 7:40; Heb 8:9). See the Book of Exodus for details of the escape.

EZEKIEL (God strengthens). Though he grew up in Judah, he was deported to Babylon with **Jehoiachin** in 597 B.C. He lived with the Jewish exiles by the canal, Kebar (Eze 1:1, 3; 3:15) and was called to be a prophet in the fifth year of his captivity and prophesied from 593–571 B.C. (Eze 29:17; 1:1–2). See the Book of Ezekiel for his prophecies.

EZRA (help). An exile in Babylon, he was sent by Artaxerxes I to Jerusalem in 458 B.C. to establish the regular observance of Jewish laws in the land (Ezr 7). A priest and scribe, he is regarded as a founding figure of Judaism. All that we know of him is contained in Ezr 7–10 and Ne 8–10.

FAITH Used to denote either trust and reliance on God or fidelity, since genuine faith in God is seen to result in faithfulness to his will. In the OT faith is response to God's revelation of himself in human history and events (Ge 15:6; 2 Ch 20:20; Hab 2:4; and see Heb 11). In the NT faith is in God the Father through Jesus, the **Messiah** (Mt 9:22, 29; 15:28; Jn 8:30; Ac 3:16; 14:27; Ro 1:5, 8). Faith is a gift of God (Eph 2:8) but given to all who seek the Lord for his salvation (Ro 10:8, 17). And faith in God brings understanding of his character, will and purposes (Heb 11:3).

FALL, THE A way of describing the loss of direct relationship with God which **Adam** and **Eve** experienced through their disobedience (Ge 3; Ro 5:12–13; 1 Co 15:22; 1 Ti 2:14). Since they were representative human beings their fall placed all the human race in a state of **sin**—not enjoying direct spiritual communion with God.

FALSE CHRISTS/FALSE PROPHETS Both Jesus and the apostles warned Christians that they would have to discern those claiming to be teachers and leaders who were in fact not genuine servants of Jesus (Mt 7:15; 1 Jn 4:1). In particular there would be an increase of these people just before the end of the age (Mt 24:11, 24; Mk 13:22).

FAMILY In early OT times a family was a tribe or a household, including cousins, grandparents, servants and slaves (Ge 46:8–26). After the Exile and on into NT times the size of the family unit became smaller, especially as people came to live in cities. Traditional duties placed on the father were provider, master, teacher and 'priest' and on the mother were household-manager and teacher. The duties of family members are seen as of divine origin (Eph 5:22–6:9; Col 3:18–22). And the Church is called the household of God (Gal 6:10; Eph 2:19; 3:15; 1 Pe 4:17).

FASTING The abstaining from food for religious purposes was required by the Law of Moses only on the Day of **Atonement** (Lev 16:29, 31; 23:27–32). Individuals were free to add to this duty (2 Sa 12:16, 21–23). On return from **Exile** four annual fasts were held to remember the days of captivity (Zec 7:1–7; 8:19). Later, fasting took place at the Feast of **Purim** (Est 4:1–3, 15–17). Jesus approved of fasting under certain conditions (Mt 6:16–18; 9:14–17).

FATHER God is portrayed as the Father of Israel because his love for this people is like (but greater than) the love of a father for his son (Ex 4:22f; Dt 1:31; 8:5; Hos 11:1). Jesus took over this usage and gave it greater significance. He spoke of God as 'my Father' and (with reference to the disciples) as 'your Father' (Jn 20:17). In fact Jesus taught that prayer should begin, 'Our Father . . .' (Mt 6:9) and he himself prayed, 'Father . . .' (Jn 17:1). Paul taught that those who believe on the Lord Jesus are adopted into God's family, calling God 'Father' (Ro 8:15). See **Abba**.

FEAR The 'fear of the LORD' is a basic theme in OT religion and means reverence for God as Creator and Judge (Ps 19:9; 33:8; 34:9; 128:1). It is an attitude towards God which recognises in particular that he is the ultimate and perfect Judge (Lk 12:5; Php 2:12). It is not eliminated by loving God but is rather lifted on to a higher plane (1 Pe 1:17; 2:17).

FEASTS A day or a season particularly dedicated to the Lord (Lev 23:2,4; Nu 15:3). Those feasts which are mentioned in the OT are: (1) **Unleavened Bread** (Ex 23:15) or Passover (Lev 23:5), an annual celebration. (2) **Weeks** later called Pentecost (Ex 23:16; 34:22; Nu 28:26; Ac 2:1), an annual harvest celebration. (3) **Tabernacles** or booths (Ex 23:16; 34:22; Lev 23:34; Dt 16:13), an annual fruit harvest. (4) the **Sabbath** (Lev 23:2–3), a weekly rest. (5) The Day of Blowing of **Trumpets** (Nu 29:1; Lev 23:24), an annual celebration. (6) the Day of **Atonement** (Lev 23:26–31), an annual celebration, and (7) **Purim** (Est 9), an annual celebration.

In the NT reference is made to a further feast, that of **lights** or **dedication** (Jn 10:22). [Each one is treated separately.]

FELIX (happy). Procurator of Judea (A.D. 52–59). In A.D. 55 he put down a riot instigated by a false messiah (Ac 21:38). Hoping for a bribe he kept **Paul** in prison for two years (Ac 24:26) even though he recognised his innocence (Ac 23:29). He left Paul in gaol to please the Jews (Ac 24:27).

FELLOWSHIP-OFFERING Also known as the peace-offering (Lev 7:11ff; Nu 7:17ff), this was a **sacrifice** offered first to the Lord and then eaten as a **covenant** meal, thereby symbolising the bond between God and his people. See also **burnt-offering** and **grain-offering**.

FESTIVAL. See **Feast**.

FESTUS PORCIUS Successor to **Felix** as procurator of Judea, and a friend of Herod **Agrippa** II (Ac 25:13). Paul appealed over Festus' authority to that of the emperor in Rome (Ac 25:11).

FIRE The expression 'an offering to the LORD by fire' which occurs often in Exodus (29:18, 25, 41). Leviticus (8:21, 28) and Numbers (15:10, 13) refers to the **burnt-offering** in which the animal is offered to God and burned on the altar before him. Fire is also used figuratively to refer to either God's judgment upon sin (Heb 12:29) or the 'fire of testing' (1 Co 3:12–15) through which believers pass.

FIRSTBORN A term used both of male children and animals. Because the firstborn of the Israelites were preserved in Egypt, every firstborn son and beast became consecrated to the Lord (Ex 13:2; 34:19). While the beasts were sacrificed to God, the children were redeemed by a payment (Ex 13:13, 15; 34:20; cf Lev 27:6; Lk 2:27). Also the firstborn son had special privileges, including a double share of the family property (Dt 21:17). Jesus is called the firstborn (Ro 8:29; Col 1:15; Heb 1:6).

FIRSTFRUITS To recognise that the produce of the land comes from God, the Israelites brought to the Temple a portion of the first ripe fruits (Lev 23:10, 17; Ex 23:19; Dt 26:1–11). Jesus is called the firstfruits of all who die in **faith** (1 Co 15:20).

FISH Fish was a major source of food in Palestine but the Law of Moses forbade the eating of fish lacking fins or scales (Lev 11:9–12). After NT times the fish (Gk ICHTHUS) became an acronym for 'Jesus Christ, of God, the Son, Saviour'. At least seven of the **apostles** were fishermen (Mt 4:18, 21; Jn 1:44; 21:2).

FLOOD, THE The deluge which covered the earth in the days of **Noah** (Ge 7; Mt 24:38; 2 Pe 2:5).

FOOD The staple diet was bread made from wheat or barley flour (Mt 13:33; Jn 6:9, 13). Fruits included grapes, olives and figs (Mt 7:16; Mk 14:20; Jn 13:26). Lentils and beans were grown (Nu 11:5; 2 Sa 17:28), honey was taken from wild bees (Dt 32:13; Jdg 14:8) and milk (making butter, cheese) from domesticated animals (Pr 27:27; 30:33; Job 10:10). Animals and fish were divided into **clean** and **unclean** and only the former were eaten (Lev 11:1–23; Dt 14:4–20); but changes came in NT times (Ac 15:20, 29; Ro 14; 1 Co 8:10; Mk 7:18–20).

FORGIVENESS An act of pardon for a **sin** committed. It is the nature of God to forgive those who are repentant

(Mt 6:12; Mk 2:7) and Jesus has the authority to forgive sins (Mk 2:10). However, God's forgiveness is related to the willingness of a sinner to forgive any who have sinned against him (Mt 6:14–15). When God forgives it is a total forgiveness (Jer 31:34; Mic 7:19; 1 Jn 1:9). All sins can be forgiven except **blasphemy** against the **Holy Spirit** (Mt 12:31).

FORTY A number often associated with testing or making a development—e.g. the **Flood** (Ge 7:17), the wanderings in the wilderness (Nu 32:13), the giving of the **law** (Dt 9:9), **David**'s reign (2 Sa 5:4), Jesus' testing in the wilderness (Mt 4:2) and his **resurrection** appearances (Ac 1:3).

FREEDOM Though used of national and personal freedom in a general way (Ex 6:6; Jer 34:9), it is also used specifically to describe what God through Christ gives to the believer (Gal 5:1). Freedom from the guilt of **sin**, the curse of the **law**, and from judgment; freedom for the loving and serving of God (Ro 6:18–22; 8:2; Jn 8:32, 36).

FREEWILL-OFFERING Personal thank-offerings, additional to the set sacrifices offered by Israelites in the **Temple** (Lev 7:16; 22:18–23; Dt 12:6, 17; Am 4:5).

FRUIT The **Law** of Moses required that fruit-bearing trees be regarded as **unclean** for three years after planting, as the Lord's for the fourth year and available for the people in the fifth (Lev 19:23ff). They were precious and well guarded (Dt 20:19–20). The word is used also in a wide variety of metaphorical ways—e.g. the fruit of the Spirit (Gal 5:22) and the fruit of lips (Heb 13:15).

FULFILMENT Often events in the NT are said to fulfil **prophecies** recorded in the OT (Mt 2:15, 17, 23; 13:14, 35; 26:54, 56; 27:9). Jesus came not to destroy the **law** and **prophets** of the OT but to fill up (fulfil) what they had taught (Mt 5:17). Some prophecy will be fulfilled at his second coming to judge the world (Rev 17:17).

FURNISHINGS In the **Tabernacle** and **Temple** the main items were the large altar and laver; the table of the bread of the Presence, the lampstand and altar of incense in the **Holy Place**; then in the **Most Holy Place** the Ark of the Covenant (Ex 25–40).

GABRIEL (God's mighty one). **Archangel** sent by God with messages for individuals (Da 8:16; 9:21; Lk 1:19, 26). See **angel**.

GAD (good fortune). (1) Seventh son of **Jacob**, born of Leah's maid, Zilpah (Ge 30:10). His descendants formed the tribe of the same name (Ge 49:19; Dt 33:20). They settled in Gilead, east of Jordan (Nu 32; Jos 22:10–34). (2) A prophet who advised **David** (1 Sa 22:5; 2 Sa 24:13; 1 Ch 21:11), organised music for use in the first **Temple** (2 Ch 29:25) and compiled a history of David's reign (1 Ch 29:29). (3) The Canaanite god of fortune (Jos 11:17; 12:7; 13:5).

GALATIA (1) The Roman province, dating from 25 B.C., in northern Asia Minor, named after invaders from Gaul in the third century B.C. (Ac 16:6; 18:23; 1 Co 16:1; Gal 1:2; 3:1; 2 Ti 4:10; 1 Pe 1:1). It contained the cities of **Antioch**, Iconium, Lystra and Derbe, all evangelised by **Paul** on his first missionary journey (Ac 13:13ff). (2) That part of the province where the actual Galatians lived (possibly Ac 16:6; 18:23). Paul wrote a short but important letter to the churches in this area (Gal 1:2).

GALILEE The most northerly of the three regions of Palestine, west of the **Jordan** and Sea of **Galilee**. Here Jesus was brought up and began his ministry (Mk 1:9, 39; Lk 4:14) and there later he appeared as the resurrected Jesus (Mt 28:16).

GALILEE, SEA OF A lovely pear-shaped lake (Lk 8:22) 13 miles long and 8 miles wide, fed by the **Jordan**. Also known as the Sea of Kinnereth (Nu 34:11; Jos 12:3), lake of

Gennesaret (Lk 5:1) and Sea of Tiberias (Jn 21:1). The waters supported a thriving fishing industry. Due to the height of the surrounding hills, contrasts in temperature give rise to sudden and violent storms (Mt 8:27; 14:22). Jesus ministered both at the side of and on the lake (Mt 4:13; 15:29).

GAMALIEL (God's reward). (1) A leader in the tribe of **Manasseh**, who assisted **Moses** in the census in the wilderness (Nu 1:10; 2:20; 7:54, 59; 10:23). (2) A **Pharisee** and member of the **Sanhedrin** who advised this **council** not to take precipitate action against the apostles (Ac 5:34; 22:3).

GATH One of the five major **Philistine** cities, famous as the home of **Goliath** (1 Sa 17:4). Later the city was fortified by **Rehoboam** (2 Ch 11:8) but fell to Hazael of Damascus (2 Ki 12:17). The site has not yet been identified.

GAZA The most southerly of the five major **Philistine** cities: it was the scene of one of **Samson**'s exploits (Jdg 16:1–3) as well as of his end (Jdg 16:21–31). Its destruction by Alexander the Great was prophesied by Amos (1:6–7; cf. Zep 2:4; Zec 9:5).

GEDALIAH The name of five men in the OT, the most important being a Judean of high rank, whom **Nebuchadnezzar** made governor of Judah in 597 B.C. He worked with **Jeremiah** but was assassinated after two months (2 Ki 25:22–25; Jer 39:14; 40:5–16; 41:1–18; 43:6).

GENEALOGY List of ancestors or descendants. The major genealogical tables in the OT are in 1 Ch 1–9 and the human descent of Jesus is traced in Mt 1:1–17 and Lk 3:23–38. The NT shows less concern for genealogy than the OT for the new people of God are spiritually born and come from a variety of races.

GENTILES Name given by Jews to all non-Jews (Ezr 6:21; Ro 1:16; 2:9; 15:16). They were admitted into the Church by **baptism**, being already placed in a right relationship with God only on the basis of genuine faith (Gal 5; Ac 10:45; 11:18).

GERIZIM A mountain of Samaria, SW of Mount **Ebal**. Here the blessings of keeping the law were recited by six **Israelite** tribes after entering **Canaan** (Dt 27).

GETHSEMANE (oil press). A garden across the Kidron valley from **Jerusalem** (Jn 18:1–12): here Jesus experienced mental agony and was arrested (Mt 26:36–56; Mk 14:32–52; Lk 22:39–54).

GIBEON Originally the chief of four Hivite cities (Jos 9:17) and became a city of the tribe of **Benjamin** (Jos 18:25). Before the building of the Temple an important place of worship where **Zadok** ministered (1 Ch 16:39–40) and **Solomon** prayed (1 Ki 3:3–15; 9:1–9).

GIDEON The charismatic leader of the tribes of Israel whose story is told in Jdg 6:1–9:6. He delivered his people from the **Midianites**, a bedouin people then holding the central area of Palestine (Jdg 6:36ff). He is a hero of faith (Heb 11:32).

GIFTS, SPIRITUAL God gives the gift of eternal life to all who believe on the Lord Jesus (Ro 6:23) but to each individual he also gives one or more spiritual gifts (1 Pe 4:10; 1 Co 12:30). There are lists of such gifts in Ro 12:6ff; 1 Co 12:4–11, 28–30; 14; Eph 4:11ff. Examples are the gift of healing and the gift of distinguishing between good and evil spirits.

GILEAD (rugged). The land inhabited by Israel east of the **Jordan** (Dt 3:13). Its conquest is described in Dt 2–3. Much later the people of Gilead fell into **idolatry** (Hos 6:8; 12:11), were overcome by Hazael (2 Ki 10:32–34) and were taken into captivity in **Assyria** (2 Ki 15:27–29).

GILGAL (circle of stones). The first place where Israel camped in Palestine after crossing the **Jordan** (Jos 4:19–20). Here **Joshua** restored the Hebrew rite of **circumcision** (Jos 5:2–9). The memorial altar of stones erected there later became a pagan shrine (Hos 4:15; Am 4:4).

GLORY Used of God to refer to his self-disclosure of his holy and pure being and character (Ps 24:10). The luminous cloud (shekinah) which rested upon the **Tent of Meeting** and **Temple** in OT times revealed the glory of God (Ex 15:11; 16:10; Nu 14:10; 16:19). In the NT the glory of God is revealed in Jesus, incarnate Son of God (Jn 1:14), particularly in his death, resurrection and ascension (Jn 17:1; Heb 1:3). Human beings give glory to God in the sense that they worship and praise him because he is LORD (Lk 2:14; Ro 11:36; Php 1:11).

GOD The whole Bible, with a variety of authors, was written in the deeply-held conviction that there is one eternal, infinite spiritual being whom we call God. His name in the OT is LORD ('I am who I am'—Ex 3:14) and in the NT Father, Son and Holy Spirit (Mt 28:19). He is the Creator and Preserver of the universe (Ge 1:1; Jn 1:1). The OT is the record of his relationship with, and his disclosure of his nature, will and purposes to, a tribe which became a people and nation (Israel). The NT describes how God as Man ministered in Palestine as Jesus of Nazareth. Thus in Jesus there is further revelation of God, particularly as having the nature of holy love (1 Jn 1:5; 4:16). Jesus saw himself as the Son of God and he spoke of his unity with, but distinction from, the Father and the Holy Spirit—thus the doctrine that God is one, but three in one (Jn 14:26; 15:26; 20:17).

References to other gods in the Bible are always to false gods (Jdg 6:31; 1 Ki 18:27; 1 Co 8:4–6) and demonic (1 Co 10:19–22).

GOG A king who in the remote future will lead the armies of Magog, Meshech and Tubal against a restored Israel: but his armies will be annihilated by the LORD without human intervention (Eze 38–39; Rev 8).

GOLGOTHA (skull). The place of the execution of Jesus (Mt 27:33; Mk 15:22; Jn 19:17), which was outside the old city of Jerusalem.

GOLIATH A gigantic warrior of the Philistine army (1 Sa 17). He was slain by **David**, using a sling and stones.

GOMER (1) The eldest son of Japheth (Ge 10:2–3) and the ancestor of the Cimmerians who settled in Cappadocia. (2) The wife of **Hosea**, the prophet, who had three children (Hos 1:2–9).

GOSHEN The part of the East Nile Delta in Egypt where the Israelites lived (Ge 47:6, 27) during their enforced stay. It was suited to flocks and herds (Ge 46:34; 47:1, 4, 6).

GOSPEL (good news). Occurring 75 times in the NT, it is used of the good news that God has caused to happen, which he promised earlier by the Hebrew prophets: the time of salvation has arrived (Mk 1:14; Mt 11:2–5; Lk 4:16–21). It is good news from God concerning Jesus, **Messiah**, Saviour and Lord (Ro 1:2; 16–17). The four 'Gospels' are so called because their contents describe the gospel.

GRACE As used of God and Jesus Christ this word points to the exceptional kindness of God towards human beings (as sinners) in making their **forgiveness** and **salvation** possible (Jn 1:14; Eph 2:4–5). And this unmerited mercy is always available to those sinners who believe the gospel and obey the Lord (Ac 11:23; 20:32; 2 Co 9:14). It became a key word—nearly a slogan—of the early churches being joined with **peace** in greetings (Ro 1:7; 1 Co 1:3; Gal 1:3).

GRAIN-OFFERING A sacrifice of flour or baked bread or plain grain (barley, wheat) with oil, frankincense and salt

(Lev 2:1–16), accompanied by wine (Lev 23:13). No leaven or honey was to be used (Lev 2:11). A portion was burnt as an offering to God and the rest was given to the priests at the Temple. In the case of poor people a grain-offering could replace a **burnt-offering** (Lev 5:11).

GREECE, GREEKS See page 43.

GUILT-OFFERING This was a special kind of **sin-offering** (Lev 5:14–6:7). The guilt involved is usually that against a fellow Israelite and thus apart from the offering of a ram in sacrifice, some kind of restitution is required, plus an extra fifth, to the wronged neighbour.

HABAKKUK (embrace). The name of an eighth century prophet responsible for the book that bears his name. Nothing is known about him.

HADES A Greek word meaning the place or state of the dead (Mt 16:18; Rev 1:18; 20:13–14). However, it is a general word and is not the same as either **heaven** or **hell**.

HAGAR (flight). Maid of Sarai, who bore a son for **Abraham** called Ishmael (Ge 16:1–16). Later, she and Ishmael were expelled from the family (Ge 21:1–21). Paul made Hagar's experience into a symbolic telling of the difference between **law** and **grace** (Gal 4:21ff).

HAGGAI (festal). The name of a sixth century prophet responsible for the book that bears his name. He lived soon after the exile in Babylon and was a contemporary of **Zechariah** (Hag 1:1; Zec 1:1).

HALLELUJAH (Praise the LORD). An exclamation of praise. The use of the word in Rev 19:1–6 is borrowed from the first and last verses of Psalms 146–150 (Praise the LORD).

HAM (1) The youngest son of **Noah**, one of the eight

persons to live through the **Flood**, and the ancestor of the Egyptians, Libyans, Ethiopians and Canaanites (Ge 10:6–20). (2) Ham's descendants, principally the Egyptians (Ps 78:51; 105:23). (3) A city of the Zuzites, east of the **Jordan** (Ge 14:5).

HAND Apart from its normal usage the hand was seen as a symbol of power ('my right hand'—Ps 110:1; Ac 2:34) and of the transmission of blessing or authority (laying on of hands—Ge 48:13–14; Lev 1:4; Mk 6:5; Ac 8:17–19).

HANNAH (grace). The favourite of the two wives of Elkanah (1 Sa 1) and mother of **Samuel**. Her song of thanksgiving for his birth (1 Sa 2:1–10) suggests she was a prophetess.

HARAN (1) A city on the main route from Nineveh to Aleppo. It is associated with Abraham (Ge 11:31; cf Ac 7:2, 4), was the home of **Rebekah** (Ge 27:43) and was where **Jacob** fled to escape from **Esau** (Ge 29:4; 29:32–30:24). (2) A personal name—e.g. that of Abraham's brother (Ge 11:26–31).

HARVEST In a twelve-month period from September to August two months were for the olive harvest, followed by five months of planting and cultivation, then two months of grain harvest, two months of vine cultivation and a month of fruit harvest. Three feasts were associated with harvest —**Unleavened Bread**, **Weeks** and **Tabernacles**. Further, the harvest is used in a variety of ways to illustrate the growth and final stages of the kingdom of God (Mt 9:37f; 13:39).

HAZAEL (whom God beholds). A powerful king of **Syria** and a scourge to Israel in the reigns of **Jehoram**, **Jehu** and **Jehoahaz**. He was anointed as king by Elisha to succeed Ben-Hadad (2 Ki 8:7–15), and reigned 841–798 B.C.

HEAD Used figuratively in the NT of (a) the husband as head of the wife (1 Co 11:3; Eph 5:23); (b) Christ as head of the Church (Eph 4:15; 5:22–23; Col 1:18); (c) Christ as head of all people and power (1 Co 11:3; Col 2:10) and (d) God the Father as head of Christ (1 Co 11:3).

HEALTH AND DISEASE The **Law** of Moses contains (for its time) a remarkable sanitary code and provision for public health (see Lev 11–15). In the Bible God is seen as the healer of diseases both in natural and supernatural ways (Ps 103:3; Mt 8:16–17) and in certain cases as the one who sends diseases (Ex 9:8ff). The use of such remedies as were known was not seen to be in conflict with belief in God as healer. The most common diseases mentioned in the Bible were: female barrenness, blindness, boils, skin disorders, consumption, deafness, dropsy, dumbness, dysentery, epilepsy, fever, inflammation, itching (eczema), leprosy, mental disorder, paralysis, plague, scabs and spots, and results of demon possession.

HEART Though a few times used of the physical organ, heart normally refers to the innermost being of a human being, both the mind and the seat of the affections (Ps 4:7; 9:1; Pr 2:2, 10; Mt 5:8, 28; Eph 1:18; 5:19). If not in communion with God it is sinful and needing cleansing (Ps 51:10; Jer 17:9–10).

HEAVEN (1) Part of the cosmos (Ge 1:1; 14:19; Ex 20:4). (2) The place where God particularly dwells and is there served by **angels** (Isa 66:1; Da 2:18–19; Mt 5:16; Heb 1:3; Rev 19:11). Jesus Christ ascended into heaven (Ac 1:11; 1 Th 1:10; 4:16) from where he will come at the end of the age to judge the world.

HEBREW/HEBREWS The descendants of Abraham through Jacob, also called Israelites (after Jacob's new name of Israel Ex 5:1–3). Foreigners thought of them as Hebrews (Ex 1:16; 2:6; 1 Sa 13:3; 14:21), and the Israelites described themselves as such to foreigners (Ge 40:15; Ex 10:3; Jnh 1:9). In the NT a Hebrew is either a Jew free of

Greek influences (Ac 6:1) or a Jew as distinguished from a non-Jew (2 Co 11:22; Php 3:5).

HEBREW LANGUAGE The language of all the OT except Ezr 4:8–6:18; 7:12–26; Da 2:4–7:28; Jer 10:11. It is a Semitic language and its sister languages are Aramaic, Arabic and Akkadian.

HEBRON (confederacy). (1) A very ancient city 19 miles SW of **Jerusalem**, originally known as Kiriath Arba (Jos 14:15; 15:13). Conquered by **Caleb** (Jos 14:6–15; 15:14–19), it was **David**'s capital city (2 Sa 5:3–5) before he moved to Jerusalem. **Absalom** later made it his headquarters when he rebelled against his father (2 Sa 15:7–12). (2) The name of several men in the OT (e.g. Ex 6:18; 1 Ch 2:42–43).

HEIR See **inheritance**.

HELL The place and sphere of everlasting separation from God and punishment by him. The word translated as hell is Gehenna, the name of a valley near Jerusalem where children were sacrificed by fire in pagan rites (2 Ki 23:10; 2 Ch 28:3; 33:6; Jer 7:31; 32:35). Jewish writers first used it to describe everlasting punishment: Jesus and the apostles took up this usage (Mt 5:22, 29, 30; Mk 9:43; Lk 12:5).

HEROD Four men have this name. (1) Herod the Great, appointed procurator of Judea by Julius Caesar in 47 B.C.; later he was given the title of 'king of the Jews' and he reigned till 4 B.C. (Mt 2; Lk 1:5). (2) Herod the Ethnarch (Archelaus) his son. He ruled Judea from 4 B.C. to A.D. 6 (Mt 2:22). (3) Herod the Tetrarch (Lk 3:19; Mk 6:14–28; Lk 23:7ff) also called Antipas, a younger son of Herod the Great. He ruled Galilee and Perea 4 B.C. to A.D. 39. (4) Herod the king (Herod Agrippa I) grandson of Herod the Great. He ruled Galilee, Judea and Samaria from A.D. 34–44 (Ac 12). His son, Agrippa II, ruled from A.D. 50 (Ac 25:13–26:32). All three ruled within the general oversight of the Roman Empire.

HERODIAS A granddaughter of Herod the Great who married her uncle, **Philip**, but later was taken as his wife by Herod Antipas. The latter was reproved by **John the Baptist** for his immoral action (Lk 3:19–20). Salome was the daughter of her first husband (Mk 6:22).

HEZEKIAH (Yahweh has strengthened). King of Judah from 724–695 B.C. (2 Ki 18–20; 2 Ch 29–32; Isa 36–39). He cleansed the Temple of idolatrous worship and re-opened it for orthodox worship (2 Ch 30). Yet he risked his **covenant** with the Lord by listening to the Assyrians (Isa 39:5–7). **Manasseh**, his son, succeeded him.

HIGH PLACES/HILL TOPS In Canaan the tops of hills often had shrines to **Baal**. On entering the land the Israelites were told to destroy them (Dt 12:2ff) but they constantly compromised and worshipped at them (1 Sa 9:14, 19; 1 Ki 14:23; 2 Ki 17:10; 23:13).

HIGH PRIEST After the exile in Babylon, the high priest was the most important person in the restored Jewish community in Palestine. He was in charge of worship in the **Temple**, president of the **council** (Sanhedrin), and chief representative of the people to the officers of the foreign powers, who ruled **Palestine** in this period. In the NT Jesus was brought before him for trial (Mt 26:57ff). And in the letter to the Hebrews Jesus is presented as a unique high priest (Heb 4:14–7:28). See **priest**.

HITTITES A people from Asia Minor and north Syria who, along with the Egyptians and Mesopotamians, were one of the three great powers confronting early Israel (2 Ki 7:6). They inhabited Hebron in the time of **Abraham** (Ge 23). **Esau** married Hittite wives (Ge 26:34; 27:46). David made use of Hittite warriors (1 Sa 26:6; 2 Sa 11:3; 23:39) and later Solomon reduced Hittites to bond service (1 Ki 9:20).

HOLY/HOLINESS God is often said to be holy (1 Sa 2:2;

6:20; Ps 30:4; 33:21; 99:3, 5) and thus places are made holy by his presence (Dt 26:15; Jos 5:15; Ex 40:9; 2 Ch 29:5, 7). Further, all that is used in his service becomes holy because of that use—**altars** (Ex 29:37; 30:10, 29), **priests** and their garments (Lev 21:1–6; Ex 28:2, 4). To be holy is to be separated from impurity and set apart for special purposes. Separation and purity are the core of holiness. Thus Jesus is said to be holy (Mk 1:24; Lk 4:34) and Christians, like Israelites, are called to be holy (Jer 2:3; Ro 1:7; 1 Co 1:2).

HOLY PLACE/MOST HOLY PLACE See **Tabernacle**.

HOLY SPIRIT The name of one of the LORD's three modes of being (Mt 28:19; 2 Co 13:14). Additional to 'Father' and 'Son'. Jesus calls him 'Counsellor' in Jn 14–16, e.g. 14:26; 15:26. He is said to come upon individuals to empower them for specific tasks (Lk 1:15, 41, 67; 2:25–27) and to dwell in believers (Ro 8:1–27). His true nature was not known in OT times; only in relation to Jesus (Jn 7:37–39; Ac 2) is his full identity revealed.

HONEY A favourite food (Pr 24:13) found in the wild (Dt 32:13; Ps 81:6; 1 Sa 14:25–26). Canaan is described as a 'land flowing with milk and honey' (Dt 6:3; 11:9; 26:9, 15). **John the Baptist** fed on it in the wilderness (Mt 3:4).

HOPE That by which we think about and picture the future. It is to be focused upon God, who has control of present and future and in whom is grace and mercy (Ps 31:24; 33:20; 39:7; 42:5). And by the influence and help of the **Holy Spirit** hope in God through Christ is given additional depth, strength and direction (Ro 5:2–5; 8:20–25; 15:13; Col 1:27; Heb 11:1). **Faith**, hope and **love** belong together (1 Co 13:13).

HORN The ram's horn was used as a musical instrument (Jos 6:5) and as a receptacle for anointing oil (1 Sa 16:1, 13). On the four corners of the **altars** in the **Tabernacle** and **Temple** were carved horns: on these sacrificial blood was smeared (Ex 27:2; 30:2, 10; 37:26; Lev 4:7, 18, 25, 30, 34). Further the horn is used figuratively of power (Zech 1:18ff). In Da 7 & 8 and Rev 13 & 17 horns represent individual rulers.

HOSANNA (save now). Originally a prayer (Ps 118:25) but used as an exclamation of praise (Mt 21:9, 15; Mk 11:9–10; Jn 12:13) for Jesus as he entered Jerusalem.

HOSEA Prophet of the northern kingdom of Israel born in the reign of Jeroboam II (786–746 B.C.). He prophesied in the reigns of **Uzziah** (783–743 B.C.), **Jotham** (742–735 B.C.), **Ahaz** (735–715 B.C.) and **Hezekiah** (715–686 B.C.) of the southern kingdom of Judah (Hos 1:1). The catalyst of his message of faithfulness to the LORD was his own marriage to **Gomer**, who was unfaithful to him (Hos 1–3).

HOSHEA (salvation). The name of four men in the OT but chiefly of the twentieth and last king of Israel (732–723 B.C.; 2 Ki 17:1–41). His kingdom was invaded by the Assyrians.

HOUR Normally one-twelfth of the period of daylight from sunrise to sunset (Jn 11:9). Sometimes the hour is a point of crisis, especially in the ministry of Jesus (Mk 14:41; Mt 25:13; Jn 2:4; 7.30; 8:20; 12:23).

HULDAH (weasel). A prophetess in the reign of **Josiah** (2 Ki 22:14–20; 2 Ch 34:22–28). She confirmed that the scroll of the **Law** found by Hilkiah in the Temple was genuine.

HUMILITY A virtue to be cultivated and admired because God humbled himself (Ps 113:5–6) and so did Christ in his becoming man (Php 2:5–11). Lowliness of mind and meekness are pleasing to God (Ps 147:6; 149:4; Pr 3:34; Jas 4:10; 1 Pe 3:8; 5:5). Jesus set an example of humility in his life and ministry that Christians are to follow (2 Co 8:9).

IDOLATRY Either the worship of heathen gods via their

idols or the worship of the LORD by means of idols of
wood or metal. The Israelites constantly fell into the latter
practice (Ex 32; 2 Ch 34:33; Hos 8:4; 10:6) and were often
near to the former (1 Ki 16:31–33). Any form of idolatry
was condemned from the beginning (Ex 20:4; 34:13,17; Dt
4:16) and the prophets constantly spoke against it (Isa 2:8;
40:18–20; 44:6–20; Ps 115:4–7). The NT follows the
emphasis of the OT in condemning it (1 Th 1:9; 1 Jn 5:21).
See **Asherah**, **Baal**, and **image**.

IMAGE A material representation of a god. (1) Images of
wood, metal and stone become idols when worshipped.
Their use was condemned in Israel (Jer 10:3–5; Hos 11:2).
(2) Human beings are said to be made in God's image (Ge
1:26–27) in that they reflect their Creator's nature; and
Jesus Christ as Man is the perfect image of God (1 Co 11:7;
2 Co 4:4; Col 1:15).

IMMANUEL (with us is God). A name given to a child (Isa
7:14; 8:8) and later to Jesus (Mt 1:23).

INCENSE Genuine incense is frankincense, a gum from
Boswellia trees, and this is what was offered to the baby
Jesus (Mt 2:11). The mixture used as incense in the
Tabernacle and **Temple** is described in Ex 30:34–38. There
was an altar of incense (Ex 30:1–9). Only **priests** could offer
it to God; fire was taken from the altar of **burnt-offering**
and placed on the altar of incense: then the incense was
poured from a golden vessel on to the fire (Lk 1:8–10). It
served to symbolise prayer ascending to God (Ps 141:2;
Rev 8:3–5).

INHERITANCE The land of Canaan was understood as the
inheritance of the LORD (Ex 15:17) and thus lots were
drawn to discover allocation for the tribes of Israel (Jos
18:2–10). The **Law** of Moses presumed that the land then
belonged to the family—the eldest son received a double
portion and other sons equal shares (Nu 27:8–11). In the
NT inheritance is understood spiritually as the inheritance

of God via Christ (the true heir) to believers of **salvation** (Heb 1:2; Ro 4:13–15; Gal 5:21) waiting in heaven (1 Pe 1:4) and guaranteed by the indwelling **Holy Spirit** (Eph 1:44).

ISAAC (he laughs). Son of Abraham and Sarah, who both laughed at the possibility of their having a son in their old age (Ge 17:17; 18:12–15; 21:6). His conception was a miracle and through him God continued the promises made to Abraham (Ge 12:1–3; Ro 4:16–21; 9:7–9). After being presented to the LORD as an offering (but never offered —Ge 22; Heb 11:17–19), he later married **Rebekah** (Ge 24) who eventually had twins (**Esau** and **Jacob**, Ge 25:22–26).

ISAIAH (salvation of Yahweh). Little is known about the personal life of this prophet who served the LORD in the reigns of **Uzziah**, **Jotham**, **Ahaz** and **Hezekiah**. He began to prophesy in 740 B.C. (Isa 6:1) and continued at least till 681 B.C. (the death of **Sennacherib** of Assyria, Isa 37:38). His vision of the holiness of God by which he was called to be a **prophet** (Isa 6) dominated his prophecies. He often spoke of God as the Holy One of Israel who required holiness in his **covenant** people (chapters 1–39).

ISHMAEL (God hears). The name of five men in the OT of whom the son of Abraham and his concubine, **Hagar**, is the most important (Ge 16:15–16; Gal 4:21–31). He was expelled with his mother from the tribal camp (Ge 21:8–21). Later he married an Egyptian and became the father of twelve princes (Ge 25:12–16). Arabs claim descent from him via Ishmaelites (Ge 37:28, 36; Jdg 8:24).

ISRAEL (God strives). Used in three ways. (1) Of the son of **Isaac** who was also called **Jacob** (Ge 32:28). (2) The people of Israel, who were descended from his twelve sons (Ge 34:7; 49:16; 32:32; Ex 1:7). They went down into Egypt, came out under Moses and settled in Canaan. (3) The kingdom of Israel composed of ten of the tribes whose first king was Jeroboam and whose territory was in

N Canaan (1 Ki 12). It lasted from 930–722 B.C. (2 Ki 17). See **Kings of Israel**.

ISSACHAR Fifth son of Jacob and Leah (Ge 30:18; 35:23) and gave his name to a tribe of Israel (Ge 46:13; Ex 1:3; Nu 26:23–24; Jos 19:17–25).

JACOB (he clutches). Twin brother of **Esau** and son of **Isaac** and **Rebekah** (Ge 25:26). His story is told in detail in Ge 26–50. He gained the birthright and fatherly blessing (due to Esau) and became the 'father' of the people Israel, through his twelve sons: **Reuben**, **Simeon**, **Levi**, **Judah**, **Issachar** and **Zebulun** (mother Leah, Ge 29:32–35; 30:17–21); **Dan** and **Naphtali** (mother Bilhah, Ge 30:4–8); **Gad** and **Asher** (mother Zilpah, Ge 30:10–12) and **Joseph** and **Benjamin** (mother Rachel, Ge 30:22–24; 35:18). God gave him the new name of **Israel** (Ge 32:38).

JAMES (1) The son of Zebedee, who with his brother **John** became one of the twelve **apostles** of Jesus (Mt 4:21). He was with Jesus at important moments (Mk 5:37; 9:2; 14:33) and was killed by Herod Agrippa in A.D. 44 (Ac 12:2). (2) The son of Alphaeus and also an apostle of Jesus (Mt 10:3; Ac 1:13), known as 'James the younger' (Mk 15:40). (3) The father of the apostle Judas or Thaddaeus (Lk 6:16; Ac 1:13). (4) The brother or half-brother of Jesus (Mt 13:55). Jesus appeared to him after the resurrection (1 Co 15:7) and he became a leader of the church in Jerusalem (Ac 12:17; Gal 1:19; 2:9; Ac 15:19–23). Author of the Letter of James in the NT.

JEHOAHAZ (Yahweh has grasped). (1) Son and successor of **Jehu** as eleventh king of Israel 814–798 B.C. (2 Ki 13:1–9). (2) Third son of **Josiah** and king of Judah for three months in 608 B.C. (2 Ki 23:33–35).

JEHOASH (Yahweh supports). King of Israel 798–782 B.C. (2 Ki 13:10–13).

JEHOIACHIN (Yahweh establishes). King of Judah for a few months in 597 B.C. (2 Ki 24:8–17; 25:27–30; 2 Ch 36:9–10).

JEHOIAKIM (Yahweh sets up). Son of **Josiah** and king of Judah 609–597 B.C. (2 Ki 23:36–24:7; 2 Ch 36:5–8; Jer 22–36).

JEHORAM (JORAM) (Yahweh is exalted). (1) King of Israel 852–841 B.C. (2 Ki 3:1–9:26). (2) King of Judah 848–841 B.C. (2 Ki 1:17; 8:16–24; 2 Ch 21:1–20).

JEHOSHAPHAT (Yahweh is judge). King of Judah 870–848 B.C. (1 Ki 22; 2 Ch 17–21). Outstanding for godliness and orthodoxy.

JEHOVAH See **LORD** and **Yahweh**.

JEHU (Yahweh is he). (1) Prophet in Israel in the reigns of Baasha and Jehoshaphat (1 Ki 16:1–7,12; 2 Ch 19:1–3). (2) Tenth king of Israel, 841–814 B.C. (2 Ki 9:1–10:36). His dynasty lasted a century—**Jehoahaz**, **Jehoram** (Joram) and **Jeroboam II**.

JEPHTHAH (God opens). The eighth **judge** (charismatic leader) of the Israelite tribes (Jdg 10:6–12:7). He subdued the **Ammonites** and then (in order to keep an earlier vow) felt obliged to offer his daughter as a burnt-offering to the Lord (11:39).

JEREMIAH (Yahweh exalts). One of the great prophets, he spoke God's word from the thirteenth year of the reign of King **Josiah** (626 B.C.) for forty years through the reigns of **Josiah**, **Jehoahaz**, **Jehoiakim**, **Jehoiachin** and **Zedekiah**. He witnessed the fall of Judah to the Babylonians and then went with his secretary, **Baruch**, and others to Egypt.

JERICHO This 'city of palm trees' (Dt 34:3), below sea level and 17 miles E of Jerusalem is one of the world's oldest cities. It was captured by the Israelites under **Joshua** (Jos 6). Much later **Herod** the Great restored the city and it was this new city that Jesus visited (Mk 10:46; Lk 10:30; 18:35; 19:1).

JEROBOAM (May the people increase). (1) First king of **Israel** 931–910 B.C. (1 Ki 11:26–14:20, 2 Ch 10:2–13:20). He led a revolt against **Solomon**, was exiled to Egypt and came back to found the kingdom of Israel composed of ten tribes. (2) Fourteenth king of Israel 793–753 B.C. (2 Ki 14:23–29). **Amos**, the prophet, had much criticism to offer concerning his capital of Samaria and the quality of his reign (Am 3:9ff).

JERUSALEM This Jebusite city in the hills of Judah was taken by **David** in the tenth century B.C. to become the capital and holy city of the Israelites/Jews (2 Sa 5). **Solomon** made it a great city through his building pro-gramme—**Temple**, palace and walls (1 Ki 4–8). In the period of the divided monarchy it was the capital city of Judah alone (1 Ki 14:21). In 586 B.C. it was destroyed by Nebuchadnezzar (2 Ki 25) but in 538 B.C. the process of rebuilding the Temple and walls began (Ezr 1; Ne 2). Later **Herod** the Great made Jerusalem into a great city again, with a rebuilt Temple. In A.D. 70 the Romans destroyed that city (Lk 21:20ff).

JESUS CHRIST Jesus (the salvation of Yahweh) was miraculously conceived and born of Mary in 4 B.C. (Mt 2:1; 13–15). He lived in Nazareth and began his public ministry after the mission of **John the Baptist** (Lk 3:1ff). This ministry was primarily in Palestine and lasted for about three years, ending with **crucifixion** probably in A.D. 33. After his **baptism** (Mk 1:10f) and period in the wilderness (Mt 4:1–11) Jesus gathered a group of disciples around him and taught them of the **kingdom of God**, present and future; of the Fatherhood of God for those who accept him as **Messiah** and of the fulfilment of the sacred scriptures in his life, death and resurrection. His primary way of teaching the crowds was through **parables** (Mt 13) and he performed **miracles** as signs of the presence and power of the kingdom of God and of his Messiahship (Mk 2:10; Jn 2:11). After his **resurrection** he appeared to his disciples and commissioned them to take the **gospel** to the whole world in the power of the **Spirit** whom he would send to them.

Information about Jesus is both in the four gospels and in the letters of the NT. The latter tell of his life and activity now in heaven as head of the Church and of his intention to return to earth to judge the living and the dead.

JETHRO Father-in-law of Moses (Ex 3:1; 4:18) who gave him valuable advice (Ex 18) on the administration of justice.

JEWS In the NT it refers to those who are members of the Jewish faith whether they live in Palestine or elsewhere (Jn 1:19; 2:6; 2:18; Ac 2:5; 6:1; 9:29). In the OT it can refer to members of the kingdom of **Judah** (2 Ki 16:6; Jer 32:12) or to converts to Judaism (Est 8:17).

JEZEBEL (1) Daughter of Ethbaal, king of Sidon, and wife (queen) of Ahab, king of Israel (874–853 B.C.). To please her Ahab built a temple and altar to Baal (1 Ki 16:31–32) and this led to a great controversy with **Elijah**, the prophet (1 Ki 18; 21). (2) A prophetess in Thyatira who disturbed the Church (Rev 2:20).

JOAB (Yahweh is father). Nephew of **David** (2 Sa 2:18) who became the commander-in-chief of his armies (2 Sa 8:16). His loyalty to and relationship with David, however, was of a mixed nature (2 Sa 12:26–31; 14:23, 31–33; 18:14–33). He was eventually murdered at Gibeon (1 Ki 2:34).

JOASH (Yahweh has given). (1) Son of **Ahaziah** and eighth king of Judah 835–796 B.C. (2 Ki 12:1–22; 2 Ch 24:1–27). (2) Son of Jehoahaz and twelfth king of Israel, also called **Jehoash** 609 B.C. (2 Ki 13:10ff).

JOB The main character of the book of Job. A man of great wealth and position he was robbed by **Satan** of his wealth, children and health. His friends thought he was being punished by God. However, he trusted in God who eventually restored to him more than he had lost.

JOCHEBED (Yahweh is glory). Mother of **Moses**, **Aaron** and **Miriam** (Ex 6:20; Nu 26:59).

JOEL (Yahweh is God). The name of nine men in the OT one of whom, the son of Pethuel (Joel 1:1), was the prophet whose book of **oracles** is in the OT.

JOHN, THE APOSTLE Son of Zebedee, brother of James (Mt 4:21; Mk 1:19), he was called by Jesus (Lk 6:14) as an **apostle** and nicknamed (with his brother) a 'son of thunder' (Mk 3:17). He is almost certainly the 'disciple whom Jesus loved' (Jn 13:23; 19:26–27; 20:2, 8). After the **Ascension** of Jesus, John was active in the church in Jerusalem (Ac 4:13; 5:33, 40; 8:14) and then in Ephesus and Patmos (Rev 1:9). His name is linked with the authorship of the Gospel of John, the Epistles of John and the Revelation of John.

JOHN THE BAPTIST Son of **Zechariah** and **Elizabeth** (Lk 1:57ff), he began his prophetic work around A.D. 27. He called for national repentance and crowds flocked to hear him: many of them were baptised by him in the Jordan (Mt 3:1–12; Lk 3:1–20). He baptised Jesus and recognised him as the **Messiah**, for whom he had been preparing the way (Mt 3:13–15; Lk 3:21; Jn 1:29–34). Later he was imprisoned by **Herod** Antipas and executed (Mt 14:1–12). He was the last of the prophets of the Old Covenant.

JONAH (dove). (1) The hero of the book of Jonah who lived in the eighth century B.C. Instead of going to Nineveh at God's command he sought to go in the opposite direction: but by a strange series of events he was required to go and preach repentance in Nineveh. (2) The father of **Simon** Peter (Mt 16:17).

JONATHAN(Yahweh has given). The name of several OT characters of whom the eldest son of **Saul** by his only wife (1 Sa 14:49–50) is the most important. He is remembered for his friendship with and loyalty to **David**, the future king (1 Sa 18:1ff; 19:1ff; 2 Sa 1:22).

JORAM (= JEHORAM) King of Israel 852–841 B.C. (2 Ki 3:1–9:26). See **Jehoram**.

JORDAN The most important river in **Palestine**, rising 12 miles north of Lake Huleh it flows through this lake and the Sea of **Galilee** and then down to the **Dead Sea**. The straight line distance is just over 100 miles, but because of its meandering its actual length is over 200 miles. Further, for most of its course it is below sea level. The Israelite tribes had to cross the river to enter **Canaan** (Jos 3:1–4:24) and Jesus was baptised in it (Mt 3:13ff).

JOSEPH (may God add sons). (1) The eleventh son and favourite of **Jacob**: mother **Rachel** (Ge 30:24; 35:24). He was sold into slavery in Egypt by his jealous brothers. Here he rose to highest office in the land and by wise planning saved the Egyptians and his own family from starvation (Ge 37–50). He had two sons, **Ephraim** and **Manasseh**, from whom descended two Israelite tribes (Ge 49:22–26). (2) Husband of **Mary** (mother of Jesus). He accepted the role of the earthly father of Jesus (Mt 1–2; Lk 1:27, 35; 2:22, 41). Probably not alive during the public ministry of Jesus. (3) Joseph of Arimathea (Lk 23:50–51), a secret disciple of Jesus (Jn 19:38). He buried Jesus (Mt 27:57–60).

JOSHUA (Yahweh is salvation). (1) Personal assistant of **Moses** in the period of Israel's journey from Egypt to **Canaan**. He took over the military leadership east of the **Jordan** (Nu 27:18ff; 34:17; Dt 3; 31). Then he led the tribes in the invasion of Canaan (Jos 1–12), divided the land between them (Jos 13), placed a national centre of worship at Shiloh (Jos 18) and caused them to renew their covenant with the LORD (Jos 24). (2) Joshua ben Josedech, **high**

priest in 537 B.C. when Jews returned from exile in Babylon (Zec 3:1–9; 6:11).

JOSIAH (May Yahweh give). The seventeenth king of Judah 640–609 B.C. (2 Ki 21:24–25:1; 2 Ch 33:25–34:1). An outstanding, righteous ruler who renovated the Temple and reformed worship. He died fighting the Egyptians (2 Ch 35:24).

JOTHAM (Yahweh is perfect). (1) Youngest son of **Gideon** (Jdg 9:5–57). (2) Son of **Uzziah** and twelfth king of Judah 740–732 B.C. (2 Ki 15:32–38; 2 Ch 27:1–9).

JOY In the OT joy is particularly associated with **festivals**, in the celebration of the relationship with the LORD, the covenant God (Dt 12:6ff; 1 Sa 18:6; 1 Ki 1:39ff; Ps 20:5; 42:4; 81:1); it is also a characteristic feature of a believer's life (Ps 4:7; 16:11; 27:6; 28:7). In the NT joy accompanies the proclamation of the good news (Lk 2:10; Jn 15:11; 16:24) and is a characteristic of the fellowship in the early church (Ac 13:52) arising from a relationship with God in Christ (Php 4:4; Ro 15:13; 1 Pe 1:8) and produced by the **Holy Spirit** (Gal 5:22).

JUBILEE Every fiftieth year in Israel was to be a year of jubilee (blowing of the trumpet). Liberty was to be proclaimed to all Israelites who were slaves; ancestral possessions were to be restored; and the land was to be rested and remain fallow (Lev 25). There is doubt whether this was ever seriously kept.

JUDAH (praise). The fourth son of Jacob: mother was Leah (Ge 29:35). He was a leader among his brothers (e.g. Ge 37:26–27; 43:3–10). He gave his name to (a) the tribe of Judah—his descendants are listed in 1 Ch 2–4; (b) the kingdom of Judah, made up of two tribes (Judah and Benjamin) and centred on the city of Jerusalem. It lasted from the death of Solomon (930 B.C.) to the invasion of **Nebuchadnezzar** of Babylon (597 B.C.). See **Kings of Judah**.

JUDAISM Used only five times in the NT (Ac 2:11; 6:5; 13:43; Gal 1:13; 1:14) and referring to the religion practised by Jews in the first century A.D. Though based on the OT it was adapted to life in the Roman Empire.

JUDAS (praise). (1) Brother or half-brother of Jesus (Mt 13:55; Mk 6:3); author of the letter of Jude. (2) Son of **James** and one of the twelve **apostles** (Lk 6:16; Jn 14:22). (3) Judas Iscariot (Mk 3:14) who betrayed Jesus (Mk 14:10, 20, 43) and committed suicide (Mt 27:3–10). (4) The Galilean soldier who stirred up a rebellion against the Roman occupying forces (Ac 5:37). (5) A Christian prophet surnamed Barsabbas (Ac 15:22–33). (6) A Jew of Damascus where **Paul** lodged (Ac 9:11).

JUDE See **Judas**.

JUDEA A part of **Palestine** organised as a district under the Persian Empire (Hag 1:14; 2:2; Ezr 5:8) and then joined with the province of **Syria** under Roman rule. It extended from the Mediterranean to the **Dead Sea** and was about 55 miles north to south, from Joppa to Gaza. Thus Jesus was born in Judea (Mt 2:1) and was also crucified there (Mt 27). See also **Galilee** and **Samaria**.

JUDGES As used in the Book of Judges and 1 Sa 1–7, it refers to military deliverers, specially called by God. They were (in order of appearance in the book): **Othniel**, **Ehud**, **Shamgar**, **Deborah** and **Barak**, **Gideon**, **Abimelech**, **Tola**, **Jair**, **Jephthah**, **Ibzan**, **Elon**, **Abdon** and **Samson**. In 1 Sa 1–7 **Eli** and **Samuel** are also called judges.

JUDGMENT As exercised by God and man it is primarily the vindication of the one who is in the right and secondly the punishment of the wrongdoer. In Israel **Moses**, **elders**, **judges** and kings exercised judgment between contending parties (Ex 18:13–26; Dt 1:16–18; 16:18–20; 1 Ki 7:7). God as Judge is said to love justice (Ps 33:5; 99:4) and acts towards Israel to vindicate people according to the terms of the **covenant** he made with the people (Dt 32:36; Isa 33:22). Thus he has special regard for the poor and needy (Dt 10:18; Ps 76:9; 82:3). Also as Judge of the whole earth (Ge 18:25) he exercises judgment in history (Eze 25:11) and will judge the nations at the end of the age (Joel 3:9ff; Da 7:9–11). In the NT the idea of a final day of judgment for the whole world becomes clearer and is linked to the second coming of Christ to earth (Mt 25; Ro 2:16; 3:6; 2 Ti 4:1). However, in the Gospel of John the present reality of God's judgment is emphasised (3:18; 5:24; 12:48).

JUSTICE (1) That standard of morality which should guide the judge in making judgment and people in relating to each other (Isa 1:17; Jer 22:16). In the OT this is the **Law** of Moses (Dt 16:19; 27:19; 2 Sa 15:6). (2) That divine concern for the right which leads God to vindicate the needy and pardon the sinner—justice becoming deliverance and mercy and also called God's **righteousness** (Isa 45:8, 21; 46:13). Paul develops this idea to produce his doctrine of **justification**—God's act of declaring a sinner to be in the right for the sake of Christ.

JUSTIFICATION The doctrine of Paul, explained in detail in his letter to Rome. There he teaches that God's righteousness/justice is revealed in the gospel for he places **sinners** in a right relationship with himself. He does this not because they are deserving of this new relationship but for the sake of Christ who by his sacrificial death made **atonement** for their sins. Thus sinners who believe the gospel are forgiven and restored to fellowship with God for the sake of Christ. In union with Christ they participate in his righteousness/justice and thus are acceptable to God.

KADESH-BARNEA A settlement in the NE of the Sinai Peninsula. Here the tribes of Israel were often found in their 40 years spent waiting to enter Canaan (Nu 13:26; 14:32–35; 20:1; Dt 1:2, 19, 46). Later it marked the southern end of the territory of Israel/Judah in Palestine (Nu 34:4; Jos 10:41; 15:3; Eze 47:19; 48:28).

KING/KINGSHIP Before the appointment of **Saul** as first king (1 Sa 8:4ff) the tribes of Israel had been led by **Moses** and **Joshua** (chosen by God and acknowledged by the people), by **judges** (for military exploits only) and then by Eli and Samuel (in the tradition of Moses). But pressure of enemies caused the cry for a king. David followed Saul and established a dynasty which lasted over 400 years (in the kingdom of **Judah**). The Northern Kingdom of **Israel** had a shorter history and various dynasties. Though kings in the united and then the divided kingdom were to maintain right worship and morality they often failed and were criticised by prophets (1 Ki 18:17–18; Jer 26:1ff); the latter also began to speak of a future king (**Messiah**) of the house of David who would be a perfect and righteous ruler (Isa 11:1–4), fulfilled in Christ (Mt 2:2).

KINGDOM OF GOD/HEAVEN The central theme of the ministry of Jesus. The kingdom is the working of the kingly rule of God in and through the ministry of Jesus. Matthew refers to 'heaven' but this is a Jewish synonym for God (3:2; 5:3; 13:11). This gracious rule which brings **salvation** in this world now will also become a kingdom (= territorial) at the end of the age. God will create a new universe after the second coming of Christ as judge of the world (Mt 25:34; 26:29; Rev 21–22). Thus the kingdom is truly that which shall be at the end of time: however, in the ministry of Jesus it is experienced as a present reality (Lk 11:20; Mt 21:31) for Jesus is (and will be) the centre of God's kingdom. In this world the kingdom is only partially seen and experienced: in the world to come it will be the whole reality.

KINGS OF ISRAEL After the death of Solomon the kings of the Northern Kingdom of Israel from 931–722 B.C. were: **Jeroboam I**; **Nadab**; **Baasha**; **Elah**; **Zimri**; **Tibni**; **Omri**; **Ahab**; **Ahaziah**; **Jehoram**; **Jehu**; **Jehoahaz**; **Jehoash**; **Jeroboam II**; **Zechariah**; **Shallum**; **Menahem**; **Pekahiah**; **Pekah**; **Hoshea**. Each one is listed separately.

KINGS OF JUDAH After the death of Solomon the kings

of the small Southern Kingdom of Judah from 931–587 B.C. were: **Rehoboam**; **Abijah**; **Asa**; **Jehoshaphat**; **Jehoram**; **Ahaziah**; **Athaliah**; **Joash**; **Amaziah**; **Azariah**; **Jotham**; **Ahaz**; **Hezekiah**; **Manasseh**; **Amon**; **Josiah**; **Jehoahaz**; **Jehoiakim**; **Jehoiachin**; **Zedekiah**. Each one is listed separately.

KORAH (1) Ancestor of a group of sacred musicians, mentioned in the titles of Ps 42, 44–49; 84; 85; 87 and 88. (2) A Levite who rebelled against **Moses** and **Aaron** (Nu 16) and was punished by God.

LABAN (white). Nephew of **Abraham** and brother of **Rebekah** (Ge 24:29). His history is interwoven with that of **Jacob** (Ge 29–31) who worked for him in order to marry his daughters, **Rachel** and **Leah**.

LACHISH A Canaanite royal city taken by **Joshua** (Jos 10:31ff): later a Judean border fortress rebuilt by **Rehoboam** (2 Ch 11:1–5). Situated 25 miles SW of Jerusalem, the modern Tell ed-Duweir.

LAMB The young of either sheep or goats (Ex 12:2–6) and much used as **sacrifices**. A lamb was offered for the **burnt-offering** each day (Ex 29:38–42) and on the **Sabbath** (Nu 28:9). Then on the first day of each month (28:11), during **Passover** (28:16, 19) at the Feast of **Weeks** (28:26–27) and **Trumpets** (29:1–2), on the Day of **Atonement** (29:7–8) and on the Feast of **Tabernacles** (29:13–36) lambs were offered.

LAMB OF GOD Jesus was called Lamb of God by **John the Baptist** (Jn 1:29, 36), perhaps recalling Isa 53:4–7 and the lambs used in sacrifice in the Temple.

LAMP/LAMPSTANDS Lamps with oil and wicks were placed on lampstands. The **Tabernacle** had an elaborate, golden lampstand (Ex 25:31ff): and in Solomon's Temple there were ten of these (1 Ki 7:49; 2 Ch 4:20; 13:11;

Zec 4:2). In the NT individual churches, shining for Christ, are called lampstands (Rev 1:12–13; 1:20; 2:1, 5).

LAODICEA A city and prosperous commercial centre in the Roman province of **Asia** (modern western Asiatic Turkey). **John** wrote a letter to the church here (Rev 3:14–22) and **Paul** mentions its existence (Col 2:1; 4:13–16).

LAW OF MOSES In the giving of the Law at Sinai, **Moses** first communicated the basic principles (Ten Commandments, Ex 20:3–17 & Dt 5:7–21) and then provided the application of them to all aspects of social and personal life, from food to worship, from property to fasting. Laws of a religious, judicial, civil and political nature are found in the 'Book of the Covenant' (Ex 20:23–23:33), the 'Holiness Code' (Lev 17–26) and throughout most of Deuteronomy, especially chapters 21–25. Jesus said that he came not to abolish this law but to bring its meaning to fulfilment (Mt 5:17). And **Paul**, following Jesus, said that to love is to fulfil the moral law (Ro 13:10). Christians are set free from the demands of the Law of Moses (Gal 5:18) for to them Christ is the end of the law (Ro 10:4): however, they are to be the slaves of Christ and obey his law (which is a fulfilling of the Law of Moses).

LAYING ON OF HANDS A symbolic sharing or passing on. On the Day of **Atonement** the **high priest** laid his hands upon the goat, **confessed** the sins of Israel and sent the animal into the wilderness (Lev 16:21) to take away Israel's sin. A similar procedure accompanied the sacrifices offered in the Temple (Lev 1:4; 3:2; 4:4). **Levites** were ordained by laying-on of hands (Nu 8:10) and so were Christian ministers (Ac 6:5; 1 Ti 5:22; 2 Ti 1:6). Further the gift of the **Spirit** was linked with this procedure (Ac 8:14–19; 9:12, 17).

LAZARUS Lived at Bethany with his sisters **Mary** and **Martha**. Jesus raised him from the dead (Jn 11).

LEAH Elder daughter of **Laban** and wife of **Jacob**. She was mother of **Reuben**, **Simeon**, **Levi**, **Judah**, **Issachar**, **Zebulun** and Dinah (Ge 29:31–35).

LEAVEN See **Unleavened Bread**, **Feast of**.

LEBANON (white). A snow clad mountain range running along the Syrian coast for about 100 miles: and the region around it (Jos 9:1). It was heavily forested, famous for its cedars which **Solomon** used in the **Temple** (1 Ki 5:6–18) and his palace (1 Ki 7:2–7). The melting snow (SS 4:15; Jer 18:14) of this range creates the rivers Orontes, Abana, Leontes and the **Jordan**.

LEVI (joined). (1) Third son of **Jacob** and **Leah** (Ge 29:34). He had three sons, Gershon, Kohath, and Merari, who became heads of families (Ge 46:11). Moses and Aaron descended from Kohath (Ex 2:1–10). A curse upon him was changed into a blessing by his father (Ge 34:25–31; 49:5–7; Dt 33:8–11). See **Levites**. (2) Levi, son of Alphaeus, **apostle** of Jesus (Mk 2:14).

LEVITES Descendants of **Levi**. While Aaron's sons served as **priests** (Nu 3:10) other Levites performed an auxiliary ministry for the priests, looking after the **Tabernacle** and then the **Temple**. Sons of Kohath looked after the furniture —Nu 3:29–32; 4:1ff; sons of Gershon cared for the coverings, screens and hangings—Nu 3:21–26; 4:21ff; and the sons of Merari carried and erected the frame of the Tabernacle—Nu 3:35–37; 4:29ff. Later in the Temple of Jerusalem their duties were expanded to include singing and collecting tithes (1 Ch 23; 25; Ne 8:7–8; 9:4–5; 1 Ch 9; 14ff; Ne 11:22ff). Various towns in the land were assigned to them (Nu 35:2–8; Jos 21).

LIFE The present life is life unto death (Ps 89:48; Ge 3:19; Job 10:9; 2 Sa 14:14). In contrast, God, the living God, is not only the giver of this physical life (Jer 17:13; Ps 36:9ff), but also giver of a richer form of life which survives death.

To those who repent of sin and believe in Christ there is true life (Mk 8:35ff; Jn 12:25; 1 Jn 3:16; 2 Co 12:15; Php 2:30). This survives death, becomes resurrection life, and is enjoyed in a new body in the new community of the kingdom of God (1 Co 15; Jn 14:3; Col 3:4; 1 Th 4:17).

LIGHT God's own eternal purity and holiness is called light (1 Ti 6:16; 1 Jn 1:5). Christ refers to himself as the light of the world (Jn 8:12; 9:5; 12:46) and tells his disciples that they are also (Mt 5:14–16; cf 2 Co 4:4–6).

LIGHTS, FEAST OF See **Dedication**.

LORD (= Yahweh). The divine name (in Hebrew YHWH with no vowels) is rendered as LORD (capital letters) and occurs many times in the OT (see especially Ex 3:14ff).

LORD Used of both God and men in the OT and translates the Hebrew, 'Adonai', meaning master (Gen 18:3, 27, 30, 31, 32; 2 Sa 4:8). In the NT used of God himself (Mt 1:20, 22, 24; 22:37), of Jesus (Mt 8:2; 20:30; Ac 2:36; Php 2:11) and of the Holy Spirit (2 Co 3:17). It is also used of human rulers (Rev 17:14). The usual word translated Lord in the NT is the Greek, 'kyrios', which was used of kings, masters of slaves, heads of households and rulers.

LORD'S DAY The expression only occurs in Rev 1:10, referring to Sunday as the special day of worship for Christians since Jesus rose from death on the first day of the week (cf 1 Co 16:1–2; Ac 20:7).

LORD'S PRAYER Not an expression used in the NT but used by Christians to refer to the model prayer Jesus gave his disciples (Mt 6:9–13; Lk 11:1–4).

LORD'S SUPPER Used to refer to the partaking of shared bread and wine (Eucharist) by the Church, as instituted by Jesus on the eve of his **crucifixion** (Mk 14:22–26). Paul called it the Lord's Supper (1 Co 11:20) and described it as taking place as the climax of a common, shared meal of church members (1 Co 11). Later this symbolic meal was separated from the full meal to produce what is now called Holy Communion or Eucharist.

LOT (covering). Haran's son and Abraham's nephew (Ge 11:31; 12:5). He became the ancestor of the **Moabites** and **Ammonites** (Ge 19:30–38). Jesus refers to him in Lk 17:28–32 and Peter in 2 Pe 2:7f.

LOVE Though the Bible refers to all kinds of love (e.g. Ge 24:67), its primary message is of the unique love of the LORD—the love of God for his creation, his **covenant** people (Israel and the Church) and his beloved Son. Arising from this is God's call for people to love him and love their neighbour (Mk 12:30–31). In the OT the love of God in choosing **Israel** is celebrated in Deuteronomy (e.g. 7:12–13) and is explained with tenderness by **Hosea** (1:6–7; 3:1f). In the NT God's nature is said to be love (1 Jn 4:16ff) and **Paul** emphasises the love of God for sinners in and through the sacrificial death of Jesus (Ro 5:5; Eph 5:25). Love is celebrated as the primary virtue in 1 Co 13.

LUKE Author of the Gospel of Luke and the Acts of the Apostles. Friend and companion of **Paul** (Col 4:14; 2 Ti 4:11; Phm 24; see also the 'we' passages in Ac 16:10–17; 20:5–21:18; 27:1–28:16). A physician by training (Col 4:14).

LYDIA Paul's first convert in Europe. At Philippi she believed the gospel and gave hospitality to **Paul**, **Silas** and **Luke** (Ac 16:14–15; 40). She was a woman of rank and head of a household.

MACEDONIA In NT times the Roman province embracing what is now northern Greece. Thessalonica, Philippi and Berea were major cities. Paul evangelised here (Ac 16; 1 Th 1:7; Php 4:15; Ac 20:1; 2 Co 1:16; 8:1–4).

MAGDALA (MAGDALENE) A town on the western shore of the Sea of Galilee from where Mary (called Mary Magdalene) came. She was a disciple of Jesus (Mt 27:56, 61; Mk 15:40, 47; 16:1, 9; Lk 8:2; 24:10).

MAGI Non-Jewish astrologers who from the study of the stars believed that a great Jewish king was to be born. Thus they travelled from **Babylon** or Arabia to **Jerusalem** (Mt 2:1–12) and visited Jesus.

MAGIC Various types were common in OT and NT times but by the **Law** of Moses it was forbidden (Ex 22:18; Lev 19:26; 20:27; Dt 19:9–14).

MAGNIFICAT Magnificat mea anima is the opening line in Latin of Mary's song (Lk 1:46–55). It is similar to the song of Hannah (1 Sa 2:1–10).

MAGOG A son of Japheth (Ge 10:2) and used of the Scythians and ungodly nations (Eze 38:2; Rev 20:8). See **Gog**.

MALACHI (messenger of the Lord). The name of the prophet responsible for the prophecies in the last book of the OT, uttered in the fifth century B.C.

MAN (= human being). Created by God and dependent upon him (Ge 1:26; 2:7ff) and existing as male and female (Ge 1:27; 2:20ff). Mortal and sinful (Ge 3) and yet by God's grace capable of being renewed (Eph 2:15; 4:24; Col 3:10) after the **image** of Jesus, perfect man (Col 1:15; 2 Co 4:4).

MANASSEH (making to forget). (1) Elder son of Joseph, born in Egypt (Ge 41:51) and brother of Ephraim. He gave his name to a tribe of Israel (Nu 26:28–34; Jos 17:1–3; 1 Ch 5:18–23; 7:14–19). (2) Son of Hezekiah and fourteenth king of Judah 686–642 B.C. (2 Ki 21:1–18; 2 Ch 33:1–20).

MANNA The basic food of the Israelites in their forty years in the wilderness (Ex 16:31–35; Ps 78:23–24). The precise nature of it is not known (cf Rev 2:17).

MARK (JOHN) John is Hebrew; Mark is Roman (Ac 12:25). Generally recognised as author of the Gospel of Mark, he was the son of Mary (Acts 12:12). He accompanied Paul and Barnabas as a missionary (Ac 15:37, 39; 2 Ti 4:11; Phm 24). He may be referred to in Mk 14:51, as the runaway young man.

MARRIAGE There is no word for bachelor in the OT and thus marriage is seen as the norm. It could be between one man and woman or one man and several women (Ge 2:18–24; Ge 4:19; 1 Sa 1:6). Sometimes a man also had a concubine (Ge 35:22; 2 Sa 5:13; 1 Ki 11:3) whose children could be given legal rights (Ge 25:6). Jesus favoured monogamy as best expressing God's will (Mk 10:1–12). Parents usually chose partners and before the wedding was the solemn engagement (betrothal—Dt 22:23–24). The **Law** of Moses allowed divorce (Dt 24:1–4) but Jesus did not commend it (Mt 5:32; 19:3–12; Mk 10:2–12; Lk 16:18). Forbidden partners for marriage are listed in Lev 18.

MARTHA The sister of **Mary** and **Lazarus** (Lk 10:38–42; Jn 11:1ff; Mt 26:6ff).

MARY Six women bear this name in the NT. (1) Mary, mother of Jesus (Mt 1:18–25; 2:11; 13:55; Lk 1–2; Jn 2:1–11; 19:25–27; Ac 1:14). (2) Mary Magdalene, out of whom Jesus cast seven devils (Mk 16:9; Lk 8:2; 24:10; Jn 20:1–18). (3) Mary of Bethany, sister of **Martha** and **Lazarus** (Lk 10:38–42; Jn 11:1ff). (4) Mary, wife of Clopas (Jn 19:25). (5) Mary, mother of John Mark (Ac 12:12). (6) Mary of Rome, member of the church there (Ro 16:6).

MATTHEW A tax collector (Mt 9:9) who became an **apostle** of Jesus (Mt 10:3; Mk 3:18; Lk 6:15; Ac 1:13). The first Gospel bears his name.

MATTHIAS (gift of the Lord). Successor of **Judas** Iscariot as member of the twelve apostles (Ac 1:15–26).

MEDES, MEDIA The old name for NW Iran whose people were called Medes. Israelites were transported there in the eighth century B.C. (2 Ki 17:6; 18:11). Later, in 550 B.C. Media fell to the **Persians** and then the alliance of Medes and Persians took Babylon (Isa 13:17; Jer 51:11, 28; Da 5:28; 11:1). Jews from Media came to Jerusalem at festival times (Ac 2:9).

MEDIATOR In the NT Christ is called Mediator because he acts on behalf of mankind towards God and on behalf of God towards mankind. He brings spiritual union and harmony where there had been enmity (1 Ti 2:5; Heb 8:6; 9:15; 12:24).

MEGIDDO A city which controlled the principal pass through the Carmel range on the important route from **Gaza** to **Damascus**. It was taken by the Israelites in their conquest of Canaan so that Solomon could build it up (Jos 12:21; Jdg 5:19; 1 Ki 4:12; 9:15ff). It was on the plains of Megiddo that king **Josiah** was killed fighting the Egyptians (2 Ki 23:29–30). In the NT the term 'Armageddon' (= hill of Megiddo) is a symbolic name for the place of a great battle at the end of the age (Rev 16:16).

MELCHIZEDEK (king of righteousness). A mysterious king/priest whom **Abraham** met (Ge 14:18ff), whose priesthood the psalmist celebrated (Ps 110:4) and who is portrayed as prefiguring Christ as Priest (Heb 5:6–11; 6:20–7:28).

MENAHEM (comforter). Seventeenth king of Israel 752–742 B.C. (2 Ki 15:17–22).

MERARI Third son of Levi, founder of one of the great **Levite** families (Nu 3:33–39; 4:42–45).

MERCY When used of God it refers to the love and compassion he shows to undeserving sinners (Ex 33:19; Ro 9:15; Eph 2:4; 1 Pe 1:3). Human beings implore God to show mercy (Ps 28:2, 6; 57:1; 143:1; Lk 18:38–39), and they are to imitate God's mercy (Mt 5:7).

MESHACH Name given to Mishael, a companion of **Daniel** in Babylon (Da 1:7; 2:49; 3:12ff), along with Shadrach and Abednego.

MESSIAH (anointed one). Though only occurring four times in the Bible (Da 9:25–26—as 'Anointed One'; Jn 1:41; 4:25) it is a very important word and occurs frequently in its Greek form of **Christ**. Jews described their expected saviour and deliverer as the 'Messiah' and Jesus saw himself as this long-expected deliverer but did not choose publicly to say so (Mk 8:27–30). However, after his **resurrection** his disciples joyfully proclaimed that he is the **Messiah/Christ/Lord** (Ac 2:36).

METHUSELAH (man of the javelin). He died at the age of 969 years in the year of the universal flood (Ge 5:22–27).

MICAH (short form of Micaiah, 'Who is like God?'). The name of seven men in the OT. (1) An Ephraimite who acted unworthily (Jdg 17–18). (2) A Reubenite (1 Ch 5:5). (3) A grandson of **Jonathan** (1 Ch 8:34; 9:40). (4) A Levite (1 Ch 23:20). (5) The father of Abdon (2 Ch 34:20; 2 Ki 22:12). (6) The name of the prophet whose prophecies are in the Book of Micah. He lived around 720 B.C. (Mic 1:2; Jer 26:18). (7) The son of Imlah, a prophet in Israel in the reign of Ahab (1 Ki 22:8–28; 2 Ch 18:3–27); known as Micaiah.

MICAIAH See **Micah**.

MICHAEL (a form of Micah/Micaiah). The patron and guardian angel of **Israel**, the Jewish people/nation (Da 10:13, 21; 12:1), an archangel (Jude 9) who fights against the **devil** (Rev 12:7).

MICHAL Younger daughter of **Saul**, wife of **David** (1 Sa 14:49; 18:20ff; 19:11–17). However, she could not understand his actions and scoffed at him (2 Sa 6:12ff) and as a punishment God caused her to have no children.

MIDIAN/MIDIANITES A son of **Abraham** (Ge 25:1–6) and his descendants. They were desert dwellers or nomads, who sometimes opposed the tribes of Israel (Nu 22–25; Jdg 7:24; Jos 13:21). Moses married a Midianite woman, **Zipporah** (Ex 2:21; 3:1).

MILK Of cows or goats (rarely camels), a part of the staple diet of the Israelites. Canaan was described as a land 'flowing with milk and honey' (Dt 26:9, 15; 27:3; 31:20). In Jewish dietary law milk and meat are kept separate in cooking (Ex 23:19; 34:26; Dt 14:21).

MIRACLE The Bible has no specific word for miracle. But it does convey the idea of God, the Lord of creation and history, directing events (often in spectacular ways) for his own redeeming purposes. The plagues of **Egypt**, the deliverance from Egypt, the giving of the **Law** at Sinai, the entry into Canaan and many other things are presented as acts of God (Ps 135–136). They are to increase the **faith** and trust of God's elect people. The miracles of Jesus in controlling nature (Mk 4:35ff; 6:32ff), casting out demons (Mk 5:1ff) and healing the sick (Mk 1:29ff) are the result of the divine presence in him bringing the kingdom of God into the everyday situation. They are illustrative of the word he preaches, the word of the **kingdom of God**. And it is recognised that **Satan** has power also to work miracles (Dt 13:2–3; Mt 7:22; Rev 13:13ff) in his attempts to deceive believers.

MIRACLES OF JESUS Man with leprosy Mt 8:2–4; Mk 1:40–42; Lk 5:12–13. Roman centurion's servant Mt 8:5–13; Lk 7:1–10. Peter's mother-in-law Mt 8:14–15; Mk 1:30–31; Lk 4:38–39. Calming the storm Mt 8:23–27; Mk 4:37–41; Lk 8:22–25. Two men from Gadara Mt 8:28–34;

Mk 5:1–15; Lk 8:27–35. Paralysed man Mt 9:2–7; Mk 2:3–12; Lk 5:18–25. Jairus' daughter Mt 9:18–19, 23–25; Mk 5:22–24, 38–42; Lk 8:41–42, 49–56. Woman with bleeding Mt 9:20–22; Mk 5:25–29; Lk 8:43–48. Two blind men Mt 9:27–31. Man mute and possessed Mt 9:32–33. Man with a shrivelled hand Mt 12:10–13; Mk 3:1–5; Lk 6:6–10. Man blind, mute and possessed Mt 12:22; Lk 11:14. Walking on water Mt 14:25; Mk 6:48–51; Jn 6:19–21. 5,000 people fed Mt 14:15–21; Mk 6:35–44; Lk 9:12–17; Jn 6:5–13. Canaanite woman's daughter Mt 15:21–28; Mk 7:24–30. 4,000 people fed Mt 15:32–38; Mk 8:1–9. Boy with a demon fit Mt 17:14–18; Mk 9:17–29; Lk 9:38–43. Coin in fish's mouth Mt 17:24–27. Two blind men (one named) Mt 20:29–34; Mk 10:46–52; Lk 18:35–43. Fig-tree withered Mt 21:18–22; Mk 11:12–14, 20–25. Deaf mute Mk 7:31–37. Man possessed (in synagogue) Mk 1:23–26; Lk 4:33–35. Blind man at Bethsaida Mk 8:22–26. Catch of fish Lk 5:4–11. Widow's son at Nain Lk 7:11–15. Crippled woman Lk 13:11–13. Man with dropsy Lk 14:1–4. Ten men with leprosy Lk 17:11–19. The high priest's servant Lk 22:50–51. Water turned to wine Jn 2:1–11. Official's son at Capernaum Jn 4:46–54. Sick man at pool of Bethesda Jn 5:1–9. Man born blind Jn 9:1–7. Lazarus Jn 11:1–44. Another catch of fish Jn 21:1–11.

MIRIAM Sister of **Moses** and **Aaron** (Nu 26:59; 1 Ch 6:3), who ensured that Moses was cared for by a princess (Ex 2:4, 7–8). Later she was a prophetess of the exodus (Ex 15:20–21; Mic 6:4). Buried at Kadesh (Nu 20:1).

MIZPAH (watchtower). The name of at least five places in the OT. Of these the most important is a town of **Benjamin** (Jos 18:26) where **Samuel** gathered the Israelites to pray (1 Sa 7:5ff) and where **Saul** was presented as the first king (1 Sa 7:5ff). Much later, after the destruction of **Jerusalem** in 587 B.C., Gedaliah, the governor, was based at Mizpah, which was only a few miles away.

MOAB Son of **Lot** (Ge 19:37) and the land, east of the **Dead**

Sea (Nu 22:1; Jos 13:32) on which his descendants (Moabites) lived. There was constant friction and warfare between the Israelites and Moabites (2 Ki 13:20; 2 Sa 8:2, 12) and the prophets often denounced Moab (Isa 15–16; Am 2:1–3). From the sixth century B.C. the Moabites ceased to exist as a nation.

MOLECH The national god of the Ammonites (1 Ki 11:5, 7) to whom children were offered through fire as a sacrifice (2 Ki 23:10; Jer 32:35). The **Law** of Moses strictly forbade this (Lev 18:21; 20:1–5).

MONEY Coins were introduced into the ancient Near East in the seventh century B.C. Before then, as after, transactions were by barter, which could make use of gold, silver or copper (Ge 23:15–16; 2 Sa 24:24). In their exile in Babylon the Jews first met coinage, that of Darius I of Persia (Hag 1:6; Ezr 2:69). In NT times coins from three sources were circulating in Palestine—Rome, Antioch and Jerusalem (hence the presence of money changers in the Temple—Mt 21:12). Though the most common Jewish coin was the **shekel** this is not mentioned, only the lepton (widow's mite of Mk 12:42). The Greek drachma (Ac 19:19) and the Roman denarius (Mt 20:2, 9, 10, 13, 19) were in common usage.

MONTH This is virtually a synonym for **moon** since a month was fixed by the appearance of the new moon (Ex 19:1). This meant that an adjustment had to be made each second or third year to fit the lunar year into the solar year. See **calendar**.

MOON Created by God (Ge 1:16; Ps 72:5; 8:3), its appearance marked the beginning of a new month and was a holy day (Isa 1:13) marked by special sacrifices (Nu 28:11–15; Ps 81:3). Often a source of idolatrous worship (Job 31:26; 2 Ki 23:5; Jer 8:2).

MORDECAI (1) A leader of the Jewish exiles who

returned to Jerusalem with **Zerubbabel** (Ezr 2:2; Ne 7:7).
(2) A Jew living in the Persian capital, Susa, and there
employed in the palace (Est 2–10). Associated with the
origin of the Jewish feast of **Purim**.

MOSES Prophet of the LORD and leader and lawgiver of
the **Hebrews** on their journey from Egypt to Canaan (Mt
17:3ff; 2 Co 3:15). A **Levite**, he became the adoptive son of
an Egyptian princess and was brought up by her while his
own people lived as slaves (Ex 2:1–10; Ac 7:22). He fled to
Midian where he received God's call to lead the tribes of
Israel to freedom (Ex 2:11ff). Returning to Egypt and
assisted by his brother Aaron he negotiated with **Pharaoh**
and eventually led his people away from Egypt into the
Sinai peninsula (Ex 4:27ff). At Mount Sinai God made a
covenant with Israel and gave his **Law** through Moses (Ex
19ff). For forty years Moses led the tribes but he never
entered the promised land (Dt 32–33). **Joshua** succeeded
him.

MOST HOLY PLACE See **Tabernacle**.

MUSIC Played a great part in community life, worship and
celebration. The **Temple** had choirs of singers (2 Ch 5:13;
Ezr 2:41, 65) and a variety of instruments were used inside
and outside the acts of worship. Stringed instruments included the harp, ten-stringed lyre and the ordinary lyre
(1 Sa 10:5; 16:23); wind instruments included different
types of horn, trumpet and pipe (1 Ki 1:40; Ge 4:21; Ps
150:4) and percussion included the cymbal, bells and sis-
trum (2 Sa 6:5; 1 Ch 15:16, 19). See **Psalms**.

NAAMAN (pleasant). (1) A grandson of **Benjamin** (Ge
46:21) and head of the Naamite clan (Nu 26:40). (2) A
military commander of the Syrian army in the reign of
Ben-Hadad who had leprosy and was cured by **Elisha**
(2 Ki 5).

NABAL (fool). A rich shepherd who insulted King **David** (1 Sa 25).

NABOTH The Israelite who owned a vineyard beside the palace of King **Ahab** in Jezreel: he was falsely accused and then killed (1 Ki 21).

NADAB The name of several men but chiefly (1) the firstborn son of **Aaron** (Nu 3:2; 26:60) who accompanied **Moses** and his father up Mount **Sinai** where they saw the glory of God (Ex 24:1–15). He became a **priest** but transgressed God's law and was devoured by fire (Lev 10:1–7; Nu 3:4; 26:61). (2) Second king of **Israel** 909–908 B.C. (1 Ki 14:20–15:28).

NAHUM The writer of the Book of Nahum, which is mostly poetry. He **prophesied** around 640 B.C. against Nineveh but nothing is known of his personal circumstances.

NAME Personal names are often significant in the Bible. God's name of Yahweh (LORD) and the name of Jesus are always significant. Names—by human intention or divine providence—often came to be significant—e.g. in terms of circumstance (**Samuel** 1 Sa 1:20), of status (**Jehoiakim** 2 Ki 23:34), of transformation (**Peter** Jn 1:42) and of admonition (**James** and **John** Boanerges Mk 3:17).

NAOMI (my delight). The mother-in-law of **Ruth** who brought her from Moab to Israel. Her story is told in the Book of Ruth.

NAPHTALI (wrestler). Son of **Jacob** and Bilhah (Ge 30:5–8) and father of the tribe of the same name (Dt 33:23). The tribe was deported to **Assyria** in 734 B.C. (2 Ki 15:29) from its territory west of the upper Jordan.

NATHAN (God has given). The name of several men of whom the most important was the prophet closely involved in the career of King **David** (2 Sa 7; 12; 1 Ki 1).

NATHANAEL (gift of God). One of the twelve **apostles** from Cana in Galilee (Jn 1:45–51; 21:2). It is possible he is the same man as **Bartholomew**, the apostle (Mt 10:3; Mk 3:18).

NATURE As used by Paul it is often qualified with the adjective **sinful** (Ro 7:5; 8:3, 4, 5, 8, 9; Gal 5:13, 16, 17, 19). Here it refers to the fact that human beings are not in their hearts, minds and wills naturally in communion with God. They need a new nature to be formed within them (Eph 4:23; Col 2:9–12).

NAZARETH A town in **Galilee** where Jesus was brought up by Mary and Joseph, where he worked as a carpenter and where he was rejected by the people after he addressed them in the **synagogue** (Lk 2:39; 4:16, 28–31).

NAZIRITE (consecrated). Separated from men because of having taken a special vow of consecration to the LORD. The nature of the vow is described in Numbers 6. For the sake of the gospel **Paul** took such a vow (Ac 18:18).

NEBUCHADNEZZAR King of Babylon, 605–562 B.C. He intervened in the affairs of the kingdom of **Judah**, destroyed the city of **Jerusalem**, and transported many Jews into captivity in **Babylon** (2 Ki 24–25; 2 Ch 36; Jer 21:2; 52:4–30; Eze 26:7–14; 29:17–21; Da 1–4).

NEBUZARADAN The general of Nebuchadnezzar's army when it besieged Jerusalem (2 Ki 25:8–20; Jer 52:12ff). Jeremiah was put into his care (Jer 39:11–14).

NEGEV (dry). The desert area south of Judea, between the **Dead Sea** and the Mediterranean (Ge 12:9; 13:1; Jdg 1:9, 15, 16; 1 Sa 30:14).

NEHEMIAH (Yahweh has comforted). Jewish exile and cupbearer to king Artaxerxes I (465–424 B.C.). The latter appointed him governor of **Judah** in 445 B.C. (Ne 2:1ff). He supervised the rebuilding of the walls of **Jerusalem** and commitment to the **Law** of Moses before returning to Persia (Ne 5:14). His personal memoirs occupy a large part of the Book of Nehemiah. See also **Ezra**.

NICODEMUS A member of the supreme Jewish **Council** (Sanhedrin) and a **Pharisee**. He visited Jesus by night (Jn 3:1–21), argued that he be treated fairly (Jn 7:50–52) and provided spices to **anoint** his body (Jn 19:40).

NINEVEH The major city and last capital of **Assyria**. It fell in 612 B.C., never to be rebuilt. Jonah was sent to prophesy there (Jnh 1:2; 3:2). **Nahum** and **Zephaniah** predicted its ruin (Na 1:1ff; 2:1ff; 3:7; Zep 2:13).

NOAH The last of the ten **patriarchs** who lived before the Flood. He was a righteous man and exemplary in his day (Ge 6:9–13). God chose him to lead those who would survive the **Flood** (Ge 6–8) after which he made a covenant with him (Ge 9:1–17). His three sons were Shem, **Ham** and Japheth (Ge 9:18). The NT refers to Noah several times (Mt 24:37–18; Heb 11:7; 1 Pe 3:20; 2 Pe 2:5).

NUNC DIMITTIS The Latin words which begin the prayer uttered by Simeon 'Lord, now dismiss . . .' (Lk 2:29–32) as he held the baby Jesus in his arms.

OATHS An appeal to God to witness the truth of a statement or the binding nature of a promise (Ge 21:23; Ex 20:7; Lev 19:12; Heb 6:16; 1 Sa 14:39; 20:23). Jesus accepted the use of oaths but condemned the careless and indiscriminate use of them (Mt 5:33ff).

OBADIAH (servant of Yahweh). The name of twelve men in the OT of whom two are: (1) The steward in charge of the palace of King **Ahab** (1 Ki 18:3–16). (2) A prophet of **Judah** of the fifth century B.C., whose prophecies are in the Book of Obadiah.

OBEY/OBEDIENCE Because God is the LORD who has revealed himself to be Creator, Redeemer and Judge, it is the duty of his creatures to do what he commands (Ex 19:5; Lev 18:4; Dt 4:1–2). Since Jesus is Lord he also is to be obeyed as God (Jn 14:15, 23, 24). Further, parents and rulers are to be obeyed under God (Ex 20:12; Dt 21:18–21; Eph 6:1; Col 3:20).

OFFERINGS Gifts (originally given by God to human beings) given to God in worship. In the OT offerings were of two kinds—of blood (**burnt-offering**, **guilt-offering**, sin-offering, **fellowship-offering**) or non-blood (**grain** or cereal **offering**, **firstfruits** of the crops and **tithes**). See **sacrifice**. In the NT all offerings are seen as fulfilled and brought to their ultimate meaning in the offering of Christ himself (Heb 7:27; 9:14). In union with him believers are to offer themselves as non-blood sacrifices to God (Ro 15:16; Php 2:17; 4:18; 1 Pe 2:5).

OIL Olive-oil (Ex 27:20; Lev 24:2; Mic 6:15) was commonly used for cooking, **anointing** (people and things), lamps and making soap (Jer 2:22). It was prominent amongst the **firstfruit** offerings (Ex 22:29).

OLIVES, MOUNT OF A flattened, rounded ridge of four identifiable summits, the highest range of hills to the east of Jerusalem. Probably heavily wooded in the time of Jesus, who often went there (Lk 19:29–39; Jn 8:1; Ac 1:12; cf Zec 14:4).

OMRI The name of several men in the OT but chiefly of the sixth king of **Israel** 880–874 B.C. (1 Ki 16:22–28) and founder of a dynasty of seven kings.

ONESIMUS (profitable). A runaway slave belonging to **Philemon**, an influential person in the church at Colosse. He was converted to Christ by Paul who sent him back to his owner with a covering letter—the Letter to Philemon.

ORACLE The word spoken by a false or true **prophet**, claiming to be a word from God through the prophet to human beings (Nu 23:7; Isa 13:1; 15:1; 17:1).

ORPHAN. God has a special concern for the fatherless and orphans (Pss 10:18; 68:5; 146:9) and the **Law** of Moses made provision for them (Ex 22:22; Dt 10:18; 16:11, 14; 24:17; 26:12; 27:19).

OTHNIEL A charismatic leader and first **judge** of the tribes of Israel (Jdg 3:7–11).

OVERSEER Used of Christ (1 Pe 2:25) and of those who have pastoral leadership in local churches (Ac 20:28; Php 1:1; 1 Pe 5:2; 1 Ti 3:1–2; Tit 1:7). Sometimes called bishops or elders.

PALESTINE (from Philistia, the land of the Philistines). Though not occurring in this translation of the Bible, it is widely used to mean the same as the territory of the united kingdom of David and Solomon, the area from Dan to Beersheba, from Lebanon to the Sinai Desert.

PARABLE A wise saying or a fictitious short story told to illustrate or highlight a spiritual/moral truth. In the OT there are nine such stories—e.g. the ewe lamb (2 Sa 12:1–14), the vineyard (Isa 5:1–7) and the vine (Eze 19:10–14). Jesus used parables often, especially when addressing the crowds: he aimed to tease their minds into reflection concerning the kingdom of God (see e.g. Mt 13; Mk 4). Some parables are in fact allegories, for each part of the story is intended to have an application (e.g. that of the sower, Mt 13:18ff); others appear to be simply stories to highlight one basic meaning (e.g. that of the yeast, Mt 13:33).

PARABLES OF JESUS Lamp under a bowl Mt 5:14–15; Mk 4:21–22; Lk 8:16; 11:33. House on the rock Mt 7:24–27; Lk 6:47–49. New cloth Mt 9:16; Mk 2:21; Lk 5:36. New wine in old wineskins Mt 9:17; Mk 2:22; Lk 5:37–38.

Sower Mt 13:3–8, 18–23; Mk 4:3–8, 14–20; Lk 8:5–8, 11–15. Weeds Mt 13:24–30, 36–43. Mustard seed Mt 13:31–32; Mk 4:30– 32; Lk 13:18–19. Yeast Mt 13:33; Lk 13:20– 21. Hidden treasure Mt 13:44. Valuable pearl Mt 13:45–46. Net Mt 13:47–50. Owner of a house Mt 13:52. Lost sheep Mt 18:12–14; Lk 15:4–7. Unforgiving servant Mt 18:23–34. Workers in the vineyard Mt 20:1–16. Two sons Mt 21:28–32. Wicked tenants Mt 21:33–44; Mk 12:1–11; Lk 20:9–18. Wedding feast Mt 22:2–14. Fig-tree Mt 24:32–35; Mk 13:28–29; Lk 21:29–31. Faithful and wise servant Mk 24:45–51; Lk 12:42–48. Ten virgins Mt 25:1–13. Talents Mt 25:14–30; Lk 19:12–27. Sheep and goats Mt 25:31–46. Growing seed Mk 4:26–29. Watchful servants Mk 13:35–37; Lk 12:35–40. Two debtors Lk 7:41–43. Good Samaritan Lk 10:30–37. Friend at midnight Lk 11:5–8. Rich fool Lk 12:16–21. Unfruitful fig-tree Lk 13:6–9. Wedding feast Lk 14:7–14. Great banquet Lk 14:16–24. Cost of discipleship Lk 14:28–33. Lost coin Lk 15:8–10. Lost (prodigal) son Lk 15:11–32. Shrewd manager Lk 16:1–8. Rich man and Lazarus Lk 16:19–31. Master and his servant Lk 17:7–10. Persistent widow Lk 18:2–8. Pharisee and tax collector Lk 18:10–14.

PARADISE A name for heaven—Lk 23:43; 2 Co 12:4; Rev 2:7.

PASSOVER This means both the original event of deliverance when the angel of death passed over Israelite homes in Egypt (Ex 12:1–13; 21–30) and the annual festival (connected to the Feast of **Unleavened Bread**) to commemorate the deliverance from Egypt (Ex 12:14–20; 43–49; Dt 16; Jos 5:10ff; 2 Ch 30:1–27). The Last Supper Jesus ate with his disciples was a Passover meal (Mk 14:12ff) and Paul called Jesus the final Passover **lamb** (1 Co 5:7).

PATMOS The tiny wind-swept island to which **John** was banished and where he wrote the Book of Revelation around A.D. 95 (Rev 1:9). It is around 30 miles off the SW coast of Asia Minor in the Aegean Sea.

PATRIARCH Father of a family, tribe or clan. In the NT this term describes **Abraham** (Heb 7:4), the sons of **Jacob** (Ac 7:8–9) and King **David** (Ac 2:29). It is used generally of the persons who are leading figures before **Moses** (Ro 9:5; 11:28; 15:8).

PAUL (little). The **apostle** to the Gentiles. Hebrew name **Saul** (asked of God) and Greek/Roman name Paul, and commonly called Paul (Ac 13:9). Born in Tarsus, a Jew of the Dispersion, he became a learned and zealous Pharisee, and opponent of Christianity (Ac 7:58–8:3; Php 3:4–6). Journeying to Damascus to root out Christians there he had a powerful vision of the resurrected Jesus and was converted to his cause (Ac 9). Thereafter he became Christ's apostle to the non-Jewish people of the Mediterranean world. His labours are described in Ac 13–28 and his teaching found in the large number of letters written by him in the NT.

PEACE The Hebrew word shalom can bear a rich meaning, pointing not only to the absence of hostility/tension but also to the positive possession of wholeness and well-being. This is seen in Ps 29:11; 85:8, 10; Pr 12:20; 14:30 and in the prophecies concerning the future **Messiah** (Isa 9:6–7; Lk 1:79; 2:14). In the NT true peace is brought into being by the sacrificial death of Jesus (Ro 5:1; Eph 2:14–15) and is made personal in the work of the Holy Spirit (Gal 5:22; Php 4:7, 9; Col 3:15).

PEKAH (opening). King of Israel 737–732 B.C. (2 Ki 15:27ff).

PEKAHIAH (Yahweh has opened his eyes). King of Israel 742–740 B.C. (2 Ki 15:23ff).

PENTECOST (fiftieth day). The Jewish Feast of **Weeks** (Ex 34:22; Dt 16:9–11), a feast of harvest and **firstfruits** (Ex 23:16; Nu 28:26). It took place fifty days after the **Passover**.

At Pentecost following the **resurrection** of Jesus the **Holy Spirit** descended (Ac 2). See **Feasts**.

PERFECT/PERFECTION There is a perfection which God possesses which is beyond comprehension (Dt 32:4; Ps 18:30; Mt 5:48) and there is a perfection (= fullest possible maturity of mind, heart and will) to which believers are called (2 Co 13:9, 11; Col 1:28). Jesus Christ became perfect (as Man) through suffering (Heb 2:10).

PERSECUTION Oppression of a group of people. Jesus warned his disciples to expect it (Mt 5:11, 44; Lk 21:12). It came via the Jews (e.g. the martyrdom of **Stephen**, Ac 6) and the Romans (1 Pe 2:12; 4:14–17; Rev 12–13). The Jews rejected the claim that Jesus is **Messiah** and the Romans would have no other 'king' but Caesar.

PERSIA/PERSIANS See page 42.

PETER (rock). Leading **apostle**, a native of Bethsaida (Jn 1:44) who worked as a fisherman with his brother **Andrew** out of Capernaum on the Sea of **Galilee** (Mk 1:21, 29, 30; Lk 5:7). Jesus called him as a disciple with the title Cephas (= Peter or rock) and this became his personal name, replacing **Simon** in priority (Jn 1:42; Mt 16:18). He is often mentioned in the Gospels (e.g. Mk 5:37; 9:2; Mt 26:37). He denied Jesus (Mk 14:66–72) but was forgiven by the resurrected Master (Jn 21:1–23). In the church he was a leader (Gal 2:9) who is often mentioned in Ac 1–12. Two letters bear his name in the NT.

PHARAOH Title of the kings of Egypt, used throughout the OT period from **Abraham** to **Ezekiel**. However, they were of different dynasties. The Pharaoh who welcomed the family of **Joseph** (Ge 37–50) belonged to a different dynasty to that which made the Hebrews slaves (Ex 1–2) and eventually agreed to their departure (Ex 5–12).

PHARISEE (separated one). A member of a minority

group within **Judaism** who saw themselves called to obey the **Law** of Moses with enthusiasm and rigour. Jesus believed that they tended to make the law an end in itself rather than as a means to an end—God himself (Mt 23; Lk 13:31; Ac 5:34; 23:6–9). Paul was a convert from Phariseeism to Christ (Php 3:4–6).

PHILEMON (loving). Owner of the slave, **Onesimus**; a member of the church in Colosse; and recipient of a letter from Paul, which is in the NT.

PHILIP (horse-lover). The name of four men mentioned in the NT. (1) A son of **Herod** the Great, whose wife Herodias left him to live with his half-brother, **Herod** Antipas (Mt 14:3; Mk 6:17). (2) Another son of **Herod** who became tetrarch of Iturea (Lk 3:1). (3) The **apostle** of Jesus (Jn 1:43–46; Mt 10:3; Mk 3:18; Lk 6:14; Ac 1:13; Jn 12:21ff; 14:8). (4) The evangelist and one of the 'Seven' (Ac 6:5; 8:5–13, 26–38).

PHILIPPI Founded by Philip II, father of Alexander the Great, in northern Greece in 357 B.C. It was the first European city to hear a Christian missionary (Ac 16). Paul later wrote a letter to the church he founded there, and this is in the NT.

PHILISTINES See page 41.

PHYLACTERIES Two small leather cases, one tied to the left arm and facing the heart and the other to the forehead of every adult Jew at morning prayer except on the Sabbath. Inside were four essential passages from the **Law** of Moses. The custom derives from Dt 6:8 (Mt 23:5).

PILATE, PONTIUS The procurator, governmental representative of imperial Rome, in Palestine holding office A.D. 26–36. He condemned Jesus to crucifixion (Mt 27:2ff; Mk 15:1; Lk 23:1ff; Jn 18:29ff).

PILLAR Used to support roofs of large rooms. Also erected to mark a holy place or shrine (Ge 31:45–54; Ex 24:4; Jos 24:26–27) or grave (Ge 35:20). In Canaanite religion pillars were associated with idolatry and so they were condemned (Ex 23:24; Dt 16:22). See **Asherah**.

PILLAR OF CLOUD AND FIRE The LORD guided the tribes of Israel in the wilderness by a pillar of cloud by day and of fire by night (Ex 13:21–22). This sign of the divine presence rested over the **Tabernacle** where God met his people (Ex 33:7–11; Dt 31:14–23; Ps 99:7).

PLAGUES OF EGYPT Ten disasters struck the Egyptians in order to persuade their Pharaoh to let the Israelites leave the country. They were unusual in their severity, their timing, that Israelites were spared their effects, and the evidence of God's particular control over them. They are described in Ex 7–12 and recalled in Ps 78:43–51; 105:26–36; 135:8–9; Ac 7:36; 13:17; Heb 11:28).

POOR, POVERTY Both the OT and NT used the concept of poverty in two related but different ways—the materially poor and the spiritually poor (humble). When the Israelite tribes entered **Canaan** to adopt a settled life, the division between rich and poor was often a problem. The **Law** of Moses made provision for protecting the rights of the poor (Ex 22:25–27; 23:11; Lev 19:9–10, 13, 15; 25:6, 25–28; Dt 14:28–29) and the prophets denounced maltreatment of the poor (Isa 1:23; 10:1–2; Eze 34; Am 2:6; 5:7). After the Exile in Babylon there developed the tradition of calling the humble and pious 'poor' (Ps 34:6; 69:32; 113:7; 132:15), a tradition known to Jesus (Lk 6:20), who also commended concern for the materially poor (Lk 12:33; 18:22; cf Jas 2:2ff).

PRAISE The joyful thanking and adoring of God, the celebration of his goodness and grace. This is fundamental to the life of believers in the OT (Ps 9:1–2; 33:2; 103:1–2) and NT (Mt 5:16; 11:25; Eph 1:3, 6, 12, 14; Heb 13:15).

PRAYER Communion with God which includes listening to his word, worshipping, adoring and petitioning him, as well as confessing sins and interceding for others. In the OT it is to call upon the name of the Lord (Ge 15:2ff; 18:23ff), to intercede for Israel (Ex 32:11–13; 33:12–16; Dt 9:18–21), to seek the face of the LORD (Ps 100:2; 63:1ff) and to confess national failures and sins (Ezr 9:6–15). In the NT prayer is the ethos of the life of Jesus (Lk 5:15f; 6:12; 9:28ff; Jn 12:20–28; 17:1ff) and is to be also that of his disciples (Mt 6:9ff). Paul's letters contain prayers (Ro 1:8–10; Eph 1:15–19) and exhortations to pray in the Spirit (Eph 6:18; 1 Co 14:14–16). Prayer is regarded as absolutely essential for all believers (1 Th 5:17).

PREACH The public proclamation of the Christian message to a non-Christian people—either Jewish or Gentile (Mk 1:38; Ac 4:20; 1 Co 9:16). The essence of the proclamation was the **kingdom of God** in the ministry of Jesus (Lk 4:16–21); for the apostles it was the crucified and risen Lord Jesus in whom the kingdom has come (Ro 1:15f; 1 Co 1:23; 15:12; 2 Co 1:19; 4:5). Preaching often resulted in persecution (2 Co 11:23–28).

PRIEST An authorised minister of God serving in the **sanctuary**. The **Law** of Moses required a sanctuary and a priesthood; **Aaron** and his sons became that priesthood (Ex 28–29; 39; Lev 8). Their basic duties were to serve in the sanctuary offering **sacrifice** and conducting **worship**, to teach the people the Law and to utter **oracles** from the Lord (Dt 33:8–11). Their dress included short breeches, a coat fitting closely to the body, woven in one piece, and a cap shaped like a cup. All were made of white linen. Unlike the **high priest**, the ordinary priest was not required to wear an **ephod**.

In the NT the priesthood at the Jerusalem Temple is said to have become obsolete because Christ is the new high priest (Heb 4:14ff) and in unison with him all believers are a new spiritual priesthood (1 Pe 2:5, 9).

PROMISE An important element in both the faith of Israel (OT) and of the Church (NT) is accepting the promises of God in faith and looking in hope for their realisation (2 Pe 1:4). God promised to Israel a land flowing with milk and honey (Ex 32:13) and a future king (Messiah) of righteousness and peace (Isa 11). To the Church Christ promised that he would return in glory (Mt 25) and that there would be a new universe created by God (2 Pe 3:13).

PROPHECY/PROPHETS Those who by words from God 'forthtell' and foretell (= prophecy) are prophets. **Moses** is the major OT prophet, called by God and given words by God (Dt 18:15–19). After him came a long line of prophets culminating in **John the Baptist** (Mt 11:3). Each one had a definite sense of call (e.g. Isa 6; Jer 1:4–19; Eze 1–3; Hos 1:2; Am 7:14–15) and believed that the word of the Lord came to him directly. Not all left behind collections of **oracles** in books (of the Bible). Alongside the true prophets there were always impostors or false prophets (Dt 13; 18).

In the NT Jesus is presented as a prophet (Mt 13:57; Lk 13:33; Ac 3:22–26; 7:37). Prophets, with **apostles**, had an important role in founding **churches** (1 Co 12:28–29; Eph 4:11). Further, prophecy as a gift of the Spirit for ordinary believers was a common feature in the first churches (1 Co 14).

PURIM (lots). A festival celebrated on the 13–15th days of the twelfth month, Adar (= our February–March). The Book of **Esther** was read to commemorate the deliverance of the Jews from the wicked Haman. The name comes from the casting of lots to determine the best time to kill the Jewish exiles (Est 9:17–32).

QUIRINIUS Publius Sulpicius Quirinius became proconsul of Asia in 3 B.C. and later the imperial legate of Syria–Cilicia. He is mentioned only once, Lk 2:2.

RABBI (my teacher). A title of honour used of Jewish

teachers (Mt 23:7) and of Jesus (Jn 1:38, 49; 3:2, 26; 4:31). 'Rabboni' is a more intense form of 'my teacher' (Mk 10:51; Jn 20:16).

RACHEL (ewe). Daughter of Laban; the second and favourite wife of **Jacob** and mother of **Joseph** and **Benjamin** (Ge 29:31; 30:1–24). She left **Aram** with Jacob to go and live in **Palestine** (Ge 30:25–26; 31:4–55) and died there at the birth of Benjamin (Ge 35:16–20).

RAHAB (broad). (1) A woman of Jericho who assisted the Israelite tribes in capturing the city (Jos 2:1ff; 6:17). In the NT she is in the family tree of Jesus (Mt 1:5) and is celebrated as a woman of faith (Heb 11:31). (2) A mythical monster of the deep (Job 9:13; Ps 89:10).

RAIN In Palestine there is usually little or no rain between May 1st and October 15th (SS 2:11). Rain comes in the spring (the latter rain, Jer 3:3; Dt 11:4) and the autumn (former rain, Jer 5:24; Hos 6:3). Not to have the latter or spring rain was seen as divine punishment (Dt 28:23–24; 1 Ki 17:1–16; 18:18). An abundance of rain meant blessing (Dt 28:12).

RAM The horned male sheep used in breeding and for priestly ceremony and sacrifice (Ge 15:9; Ex 29; Nu 7).

RAMAH (height). The name of five places in the OT. That referred to concerning the infancy of Jesus in Mt 2:18 (= Jer 31:15) is probably Ramah of Benjamin (1 Ki 15:16–17; Isa 10:28–32).

REBEKAH (or Rebecca). Daughter of Bethuel, sister of Laban, wife of **Isaac**, and mother of **Esau** and **Jacob** (Ge 22:20–24; 24:24).

RECONCILE To cause a relationship to be harmonious, peaceful and righteous. (1) Used of what disciples must do one for another (Mt 5:24; Lk 12:58). (2) Used of what God has achieved in the sacrificial death and **resurrection** of Jesus, uniting sinners to a holy God (Ro 5:10; 2 Co 5:18). (3) Used of the duty of a **sinner** with respect to God—to accept his **forgiveness** and be in a right relationship (2 Co 5:20).

RED SEA The water crossed by the Israelites as they left Egypt (Ex 10:19; 13:18; 15:4, 22; Nu 33:11).

REDEEM/REDEMPTION To release on the payment of a price—deliverance by a costly method. Used of the action of God in redeeming/delivering Israel from slavery in Egypt in order to place them in the land of promise (Ex 6:6; 15:13; Ps 77:14–15). Used also of the action of God in Christ who by his sacrificial death redeemed/liberated sinners from the guilt and power of sin (Mk 10:45; Ro 3:24; Eph 1:7; 1 Pe 1:18–19).

REHOBOAM (expansion of the people). Son of **Solomon** and Naamah who became the last king of a united Israel and then the first king of the new southern kingdom. (1 Ki 12; 2 Ch 10–12).

REJOICE To rejoice (have joyful confidence in) the LORD (Ps 64:10; Php 4:4) is a basic element in the life of a believer. See **Joy**.

REMEMBER/REMEMBRANCE A key element in Israelite religion was the act of remembering (and retelling) the story of God's mighty acts (e.g. the Exodus) for Israel (Dt 5:15; 8:2) and the content of his holy **Law** (Ex 20:8; Nu 15:39–40; Ps 119:52) in order rightly to worship and serve him. In the NT Jesus urged his disciples to remember his words (Jn 15:20) and his sacrificial death (1 Co 11:24–25).

REMNANT The spiritual kernel of the Israelite people who (in each period) remain faithful to the LORD while the majority depart from him (Isa 17:3; 10:20–22; 11:11, 16; Zep 2:4–7; Zec 8:1–8; Ro 9:27; 11:5).

REPENT, REPENTANCE. Turning from sin towards God in order to trust, love and obey him as LORD. Its need emphasised by **John the Baptist** (Mt 3:8–11; Lk 3:3–8), by Jesus (Mt 4:17; Mk 1:15; Lk 5:32) and the first preachers of the churches (Ac 2:38; 3:19; 17:30; 26:20).

REST Used in many ways but particularly of the seventh day, the **Sabbath** (Ge 2:2; Ex 16:23; 31:15) and the seventh year (Lev 25:4–5) and of the future age of the kingdom of God (Heb 4). The rest is not merely from work but into the gracious care of God.

RESURRECTION The raising from death of the physical body either in the same state as before death (e.g. as with **Lazarus**, Jn 11) or with a new, transformed body (as with Jesus, Mt 28; Mk 16; Lk 24; Jn 20–21). In the OT belief in the future resurrection of bodies at the end of the age is only found in Isa 26:19 and Da 12:2. In the NT Jesus spoke of future resurrection (Jn 5:25, 28–9) for all as well as his own specific resurrection after three days (Mk 8:31). After the actual resurrection of Jesus, the fact of his resurrection and the future resurrection into eternal life with God in the **kingdom of heaven** were basic elements in Christian teaching (Ac 2:31; 4:2, 33; Php 3:10–11).

REUBEN Oldest son of **Jacob**; mother Leah (Ge 29:32). He took four sons with him into Egypt (Ge 46:9) and when Israel left that land, his tribe had 46,500 members (Nu 1:21; 2:10). They settled in Gilead (Nu 32) and were taken into captivity centuries later by **Tiglath-Pileser** of Assyria (1 Ch 5:25–26).

REVEAL, REVELATION Fundamental to all religion in both OT and NT is the belief that God first discloses himself—his character, will and purposes—in order to establish the possibility of a right relationship with himself (Ps 147:19). In the OT the primary method of self-disclosure is via the living word given to Moses and the prophets (Isa 22:14; Am 3:7; 4:13). In the NT God is

revealed in and through Jesus Christ—his person, actions
and words (Lk 2:32; 10:22; Jn 1:31; 2:11; Gal 1:16). At the
end of the age with the second coming of Jesus in glory,
God will reveal more of himself (Isa 40:5; 2 Th 1:7; 1 Pe
1:5).

REWARD Jesus spoke of rewards in heaven for those who
are faithful in their duties to God (Mt 5:12, 46; 6:1, 2, 4, 5,
6, 16, 18). However, the precise nature of the reward is not
explained.

RICH, RICHES To have great wealth can be a sign of
God's blessing (Ps 112:1, 3). Yet wealth is from God and to
be used rightly (Dt 8:17–18; Hos 2:8; Lk 16:11). It is wrong
to trust in riches (Ps 52:7; Mk 10:23, 27); the love of money
is a root of evil (1 Ti 6:10). Spiritual wealth and riches are to
be preferred to material ones (Lk 12:33; 16:11).

RIGHTEOUS, RIGHTEOUSNESS As used of human
beings it can mean a state of innocence (Ge 6:9), of being in
the right before the **Law** of Moses (Ps 5:12; 11:5; 37:21, 25,
29) and of being placed in a right relationship with God (Ge
15:6; Ro 1:17). The latter meaning is especially developed
by Paul in Galatians and Romans: through Christ the
righteous one God declares believing sinners to be righteous in his sight (Ro 3–8; Gal 3). The theme of declaring
sinners righteous is developed from Isa 40–66 where God's
righteousness is presented as his saving activity on behalf of
Israel to place them in the right with himself.

ROME, ROMAN EMPIRE See page 43.

RUTH The girl from Moab who accompanied her mother-
in-law, Naomi, to Bethlehem and there married **Boaz** (Ru
3–4). Through her son, Obed, she became an ancestress of
King David (Mt 1:5).

SABBATH The seventh day of the week in the Israelite
calendar; a regular holy day with obligatory rest from

normal work (Ge 2:1–3; Ex 20:8–10; Lev 16:31; 23:1–3; Dt 5:12–15). Its observance became a distinctive mark of Judaism and Jesus taught that 'the Sabbath was made for man and not man for the Sabbath' (Mk 2:27). Christian Jews kept it but Christian Gentiles did not. Hebrews 4 teaches that the true Sabbath is the 'resting in God' in the life of the future kingdom of God.

SACRIFICE(S) In the **Law** of Moses the offering to God of oxen, sheep, goats and pigeons to be killed and then either eaten before the Lord or consumed by fire is central. There was the sin-offering (Lev 4:1–35; 6:24–30), the **guilt-offering** (Lev 5:14–6:7), the **burnt-offering** (Lev 1) and the **fellowship-offering** (Lev 3). Each day in the **Temple** animals were sacrificed to be burnt-offerings to God (Ex 29:38–42; Nu 28:3–8). They were accompanied by offerings of cereal/grain. See **offerings**.

SADDUCEES The name comes from **Zadok**, **high priest** in the time of king David. A small Jewish grouping of generally wealthy men belonging to priestly families. They held to the literal truth of the Hebrew Bible (= OT) and denied the future **resurrection** of the dead (Ac 23:6–10). Though they had fundamental disagreements with the **Pharisees** concerning the interpretation of the **Law** of Moses, they joined with them to oppose Jesus (Mt 22:23–33).

SAINTS Those who trust in the LORD and are set apart to serve and worship him either according to the Law of Moses (Ps 30:4; 31:23; Da 7:18–27) or in the name of Jesus (Ro 1:7; 8:27; 15:25; Jude 3).

SALVATION The God of the Bible is pre-eminently the Lord who saves. What his salvation includes and means grows in scope and clarity from the OT to the NT. It can mean victory in battle, recovery from illness, relief of the poor and needy (Ex 14:30; Ps 7:1; 18:3, 19; 59:2; 72:4; 1 Ch 16:35; 2 Ch 32:11), all in the context of God's election of Israel. It begins also to mean God's creating of a new Israel, new **Zion**, new world based on new revelation from the Lord (Isa 40–60), and there is the developing hope of the **Messiah**, the agent of God's salvation (Isa 52:13–53:12). In the NT salvation is from God and centred on Jesus: it includes physical and spiritual healing, forgiveness of sins, the gift of eternal life, adoption as a child of God and the gift of the indwelling Spirit. Salvation is what God has done in the death and resurrection of Jesus, is doing now in the work of the Spirit, and will do in creating the new world of the kingdom of God (Mt 1:21; 19:25; 24:22; Lk 1:77; Ro 13:11; Tit 3:5; 1 Pe 2:2).

SAMARIA Used in three ways. (1) As the capital of the kingdom of Israel from the time of **Omri** until its fall in 721 B.C. to the Assyrians. Rebuilt by **Herod** the Great (1 Ki 16:24; 2 Ki 17:3–6; Isa 7:9; 8:4). (2) Of the territory occupied by the ten tribes who made up the kingdom of Israel (1 Ki 13:32; 2 Ki 17:24). (3) A district of central Palestine under Roman administration (Lk 17:11; Jn 4:4; Ac 8:5).

SAMARITANS Originally used of people living in the Northern Kingdom of Israel (2 Ki 17:24f; Ezr 4:1–23). Later used of inhabitants of central Palestine who were not of pure Israelite stock but who nevertheless held to the Books of Moses and looked for the **Messiah** (Jn 4:4ff; Ac 8:5–6).

SAMSON One of the **judges** of the tribes of Israel in their warfare with the Philistines, and famous for his great strength (Jdg 13–16). Though a man of many failings, he is portrayed as a person of true faith (Heb 11:32).

SAMUEL (the name of God). The earliest of the **prophets** of Israel (after Moses) and the last of the 'judges'. He was dedicated to the service of God by his mother **Hannah** and assisted **Eli**, the **high priest**, in the **sanctuary** at Shiloh (1 Sa 1–4). He anointed the first two kings of Israel, **Saul** and **David** (1 Sa 7–16; 18–24; 25:1).

SANCTIFY To set apart a person to serve God in holiness and love. God himself sanctifies his people (Jn 17:17, 19; 1 Th 5:23; 2 Th 2:13; 1 Pe 1:2). Those being sanctified are **saints**.

SANCTUARY Usually the Tabernacle or Temple or the inner part of each called the **Most Holy Place** (Ex 36:1–6; Lev 4:6; Nu 3:10; 1 Ch 22:19; Ps 20:2). Other sanctuaries existed—e.g. at Shiloh (1 Sa 1–2).

SANHEDRIN (council). The highest assembly or **Council** of the Jews comprising seventy-one members. In the time of Jesus it met twice-weekly in Jerusalem and had both political and religious functions (Mt 26:59; Ac 5:21, 27; 23:1). Jesus was brought before it (Mt 26:59) as were apostles (Ac 4:15; 5:27), **Stephen** (Ac 6:12) and **Paul** (Ac 23:1).

SARAH, SARAI (princess). Wife of **Abraham** and mother of **Isaac**: her name was changed from Sarai to Sarah when she received God's promise of the birth of Isaac (Ge 11–12; 16:1–18:15; 20–21).

SATAN (adversary). The **devil**, a disobedient angel who opposes God's will for mankind but who is allowed by God to oppose him until the end of the age. In the Book of Job, Satan is the angel who accuses Job before God (Job 1:6ff); but by the time of Jesus Satan was seen not merely as the accuser but also the troubler of mankind. Jesus saw himself in open conflict with Satan (Lk 4:1–13; 22:53; Mt 12:26) and as inflicting upon him a deadly blow by his sacrificial death and resurrection (Jn 16:11). However, Satan is still active tempting Christians and opposing Christ's cause (Eph 4:27; 6:12; 1 Pe 5:8; Rev 12:12; 20:7).

SAUL (asked of God). (1) The first king of **Israel**. Reckoned to be the tallest and handsomest man in Israel, as well as a great warrior, he was anointed king by Samuel (1 Sa 9ff). His reign, which began well, deteriorated and Samuel anointed David as king to succeed him (1 Sa 13ff). (2) The name of the first Christian apostle to the Gentiles, also known as **Paul** (Ac 7:58; 13:9).

SAVIOUR The Lord God is Saviour (2 Sa 22:47; 1 Ch 16:35; Ps 27:9; Lk 1:47; 1 Ti 1:1; 2:3) as also is Jesus Christ (Lk 2:11; Ac 13:23; Php 3:20). See **salvation**.

SCAPEGOAT The second of two goats for which lots were cast on the Day of **Atonement** (Lev 16:8–26). The first was sacrificed as a sin-offering but the second was the scapegoat. The people's sins were transferred to it by the laying-on of hands and then it was sent out into the wilderness.

SCRIBES Official Jewish interpreters of the Law of Moses and often called lawyers (Mt 22:35) who looked to Ezra as their ideal (Ne 8:1–9). They are called 'teachers of the law' in the NT (Mt 23:2–29; Lk 5:17, 21, 30), and were particularly associated with the **Pharisees**.

SCRIPTURE(S) Used in the NT of the collection of holy books which the Jews, Jesus and the first Christians regarded as containing God's written word to mankind (2 Ti 3:16; Jas 2:8). Today we call it the OT. Jesus saw himself as fulfilling the promises in Scripture concerning the **Messiah** (Lk 4:21; Jn 7:38; 20:9; Ac 1:16). Later it came to mean the whole Bible—OT and NT.

SCROLL The roll was the usual form of a book in the times of the OT and NT. Made of papyrus or the smoothed skins of animals (Jer 36; Lk 4:17; Rev 1:11).

SEAL A device bearing a design or name (e.g. of a deity or king) so that it can leave an impression upon clay or wax (Ex 28:11, 21, 36; 1 Ki 21:8; Est 8:8). Used figuratively of the impression made upon the heart by the Holy Spirit (2 Co 1:22; Eph 1:13; 4:30).

SEER One who looks into the future to foresee events: a

prophet (1 Sa 9:9) like **Samuel** (1 Sa 10:19). Kings employed them to assist them in making decisions about foreign alliances (2 Sa 24:11; 2 Ch 29:25; 35:15). Like prophets there were both false and true seers.

SELAH A term occurring 71 times in the Psalms (e.g. Ps 3:2, 4, 8) and also in Hab 3:3, 9, 13 of unknown meaning.

SENNACHERIB Assyrian king (705–681 B.C.) who invaded **Judah** (2 Ki 18:13–19:17; 2 Ch 32:1–22; Isa 36:1–37:38) but was unable to take **Jerusalem** when **Hezekiah** was king.

SERMON ON THE MOUNT Name commonly given to the teaching of Jesus in Matthew 5–7.

SERPENT In the Garden of **Eden**, **Adam** and **Eve** were tempted by a serpent (Ge 3:1–14) speaking for the devil (Rev 12:9). Isaiah referred to a mythical serpent, Leviathan (27:1).

SERVANT, SERVE Servants were common in both OT and NT times (Ru 2:8–23; Pr 27:27). Prophets, kings and priests with others were called servants of God (Jos 8:21; 2 Ch 1:3; 6:15–21) and Israel itself was called the servant of the **LORD** (Isa 41:8). Isaiah describes a special servant of the LORD who suffers for his people and is vindicated by God (52:13–53:12; cf 42:1–4; 49:1–6; 50:4–9). In the NT all Christians are called to be servants of God in name and practice (Ro 1:9; 12:7–11; Col 3:24).

SETH (substitute). Adam and Eve's third son, a substitute for **Abel** (Ge 4:25–5:8). **Noah** was descended from him (1 Ch 1:1).

SHADRACH The Babylonian name given to Hananiah. A captive in Babylon with **Daniel**, along with **Meshach** and **Abednego** (Da 1:7; 2:49; 3:12–30).

SHALLUM (recompense). The name of fifteen men in the OT including the sixteenth king of Israel, who only reigned for one month (2 Ki 15:10–14) in 752 B.C.

SHALMANESER V King of Assyria (726–722 B.C.) who invaded the kingdom of Israel (2 Ki 17:3–5; 18:9–11).

SHEBA (1) The land in SW Arabia (eastern part of modern Yemen) whose queen visited **Solomon** (1 Ki 10:1ff; 2 Ch 9:1ff) probably to negotiate a trade agreement. (2) The name of various individuals in the OT (e.g. 1 Ch 5:13). (3) A city in Southern Palestine (Jos 19:2).

SHECHEM (shoulder). Name of a city and the prince of it in the hill country of north central Palestine (Ge 33–34). It was the first place in **Canaan** that God appeared to Abraham (Ge 12:6–7). When the tribes of Israel entered Canaan it was allocated to Ephraim (Jos 17:7) and here **Joshua** made his farewell speech (Jos 24). Later **Rehoboam** was made king here (1 Ki 12:1) and **Jeroboam** made the city his capital (1 Ki 12:25).

SHEEP The animal most often mentioned in the Bible (Ge 29; Ex 22:1; Ps 23). Kept for its milk (to make curds) rather than for meat, which was only available when the animals were sacrificed according to the **Law** (Lev 1:10–13; 3:6–11). Tanned skins were used for cloth (Ex 25:5). Jesus spoke of himself as the Shepherd and his disciples as sheep (Jn 10:1–21).

SHEKEL Until the latter part of the OT period shekel meant a particular weight of silver or other precious metal, not a coin (Ex 30:13–15; Nu 7:13ff). By NT times it denoted a coin. See **money**.

SHEPHERD Shepherds and their flocks were a common sight in Palestine (Ge 46:32, 34; 47:3). Further, God is presented as the Shepherd of Israel (Ge 49:24; Ps 23:1; 80:1). Christ is also the Shepherd (Jn 10:1ff; Heb 13:20;

1 Pe 2:25). Faithless spiritual shepherds are denounced (Eze 34; Jer 23:1–4; 25:32–38).

SHESHBAZZAR See **Zerubbabel**.

SHILOH A city on an isolated hill east of the highway from **Bethel** to **Shechem** (Jdg 21:19). Here the tribes of Israel assembled after the first phase of the conquest of **Canaan** to set up the **Tabernacle** and thereby make Shiloh the centre for worship. Here the **Ark** of the Lord remained until the days of Samuel when the Philistines removed it (1 Sa 4:3). When **David** made **Jerusalem** the capital Shiloh lost importance.

SIDON A walled city and port in ancient Phoenicia (now Lebanon) with twin harbours and divided into Greater Sidon (Jos 11:8; 19:28) and Lesser Sidon. It was able to resist Israel (Jdg 10:12) but **Jeremiah** foretold its fall in 587 B.C. (Jer 25:22; 27:3; 47:4). Much later Jesus was in or near the city (Mk 7:24–31; 3:8; Lk 6:17; 10:13–14) and **Paul** visited the city (Ac 27:3). By this time the inhabitants were mostly Greek (Mk 7:26).

SIGN An act of God which reveals his presence (Ex 4:28; Dt 4:34; 7:19; Ro 15:19; Heb 2:4). Used in John's Gospel specially of the miracles of Jesus (2:11; 6:2; 11:47).

SILAS A leader in the church of Jerusalem who had the gift of **prophecy** (Ac 15:22, 32). He was sent to Antioch and from there accompanied **Paul** as a missionary (Ac 15:36–41). His name appears in several letters (2 Co 1:19; 1 Th 1:1; 2 Th 1:1; 1 Pe 5:12).

SILVER The commonest precious metal available in Palestine and often mentioned in the OT (Ge 13:2; Ps 12:6; 66:10; SS 1:11; 3:10; 8:9, 11). Used instead of money and weighed in **shekels**.

SIMEON (1) The second son of **Jacob** and Leah

(Ge 29:33), who massacred Hivites (Ge 34:24–31) and went down into Egypt with his family (Ge 46:10; 49:5; Ex 1:2; 6:15). (2) The descendants of Simeon, the Israelite tribe (Nu 1:22–23; 26:14; Dt 27:12; Jos 19:1–9) which left Egypt and settled in Canaan. (3) An ancestor of Jesus (Lk 3:30). (4) A man of Jerusalem who held the baby Jesus in his arms and uttered the **Nunc Dimittis** (Lk 2:25–35). (5) A Christian of Antioch (Ac 13:1–2).

SIMON A later form of Simeon. (1) The apostle whom Jesus called **Peter** (Mt 16:16; Lk 5:8; Jn 6:68; 13:6, 9, 36; 2 Pe 1:1). (2) A disciple of Jesus called the zealot (Mt 10:4; Mk 3:18; Lk 6:15; Ac 1:13). (3) A brother or half-brother of Jesus (Mt 13:55; Mk 6:3). (4) A leper of Bethany (Mt 26:6; Mk 14:3). (5) The man of Cyrene who carried Jesus' cross (Mk 15:21). (6) A Pharisee (Lk 7:40). He may be the same as No 4. (7) Simon Iscariot, father of **Judas Iscariot** (Jn 6:71; 12:4; 13:2). (8) A sorcerer (Ac 8:9ff). (9) A leather worker of Joppa (Ac 9:43; 10:6, 32).

SIN The moral deviation and distortion in human beings which is offensive to God and prevents true fellowship with him. In the OT a cluster of words convey the character of sin as deliberate and wilful action contrary to God's known will as expressed in his Law. Sin is thus found in individuals, tribes and nations. Its origin is in the disobedience of **Adam** and **Eve** (Ge 3) and it is denounced by prophets (Jer 9:3; Eze 4:6, 17) and **atonement** for it provided by the **sacrifices** of the Law (Lev 4:3; Nu 7:16ff). God sent his Son into the world because of sin (Jn 1:29). Jesus as the Son of God is the friend of sinners who comes to save them (Lk 5:30, 32; 7:34). He takes away both the guilt and the power of sin in the heart (Ro 6:2; 1 Jn 3:6, 9; 5:18) through the gift of the Spirit (Ro 8).

SIN, DESERT OF A wilderness through which the Israelites passed on their journey from Elim to Mount Sinai (Ex 16:1; 17:1; Nu 33:11–12).

SINAI (1) A wilderness area near to Mount Sinai somewhere between the Gulf of Aqaba and Suez. The area where **Israel** came in the third month after leaving Egypt (Ex 19:1–2; Nu 1:1, 19). (2) A holy mountain where God spoke to **Moses** and gave him the Law for Israel (Ex 19:11ff; 31:18; 34:2, 4, 29, 32; Gal 4:24–25). Also known as Mount Horeb (Dt 1:2, 6). Probably that which is now called Jebel Mûsa.

SKULL, THE PLACE OF THE Where Jesus was crucified (Mt 27:33; Mk 15:22; Lk 23:33; Jn 19:17). Also known as **Calvary**, **Golgotha**.

SLAVES/SLAVERY Someone owned by another person. Israelites were slaves in Egypt and were never to forget (Ex 13:3, 14; Dt 15:15; 16:12). Throughout the OT and NT period slavery was common. A person became a slave for one of various reasons—capture in war, purchase, being born to a slave, selling oneself, abduction. The **Law** of Moses gave instructions concerning slavery (Ex 21; Lev 25) and Paul gave instructions to household slaves (Col 3:22; 1 Ti 6:1–3). Slavery is also used of the spiritual realm: sinners are slaves to sin and through conversion are to become slaves to God (Ro 6).

SODOM One of the 'cities of the plain' along with Admah, Gomorrah, Zeboiim, and Zoar (Ge 13:10ff; 14:2ff; 19:16ff). Because of the episode of Ge 19 Sodom became a name for vice, infamy and judgment (Isa 1:9–10; Jer 23:14; Eze 16:46; Mt 10:15; Lk 17:29).

SOLOMON Third and last king of a united Israel 971–931 B.C. Son of **David** and **Bathsheba** (2 Sa 12:24). In his reign the kingdom achieved its greatest geographical and material prosperity (1 Ki 1–11; 2 Ch 8–9). He was a wise man (see Pr 10:1–22:16; 25:1–29:27) and he built a great Temple for the LORD (1 Ki 5ff). Yet his harsh policies of taxation and his allowing of worship of idols (to please his foreign wives) led to the division of the kingdom after his death (1 Ki 11:1–13).

SON Used often in its everyday sense but also used in a spiritual manner of: (1) **Israel** as God's 'firstborn son' (Ex 4:22; Ro 9:4) and of Israelites as the sons of God (Dt 14:1–2), because of the **covenant** God made with the people. (2) **David** as God's special Israelite (Ps 2:7) whose descendant would be the **Messiah** and Son of God (Mt 1:1; 22:42). (3) Being like God in character as his **disciple** (Lk 6:35; Mt 5:9, 45). (4) Jesus as the unique Son (Ro 8:3, 32; Gal 4:4; Heb 2:10–17). (5) Believers in Jesus as adopted children of God, born of his **Spirit** (Ro 8:15f; Gal 4:6f; Jn 1:12; 1 Jn 3–4).

SON OF MAN Jesus often referred to himself by this expression (Mk 2:10, 27–28; Mt 12:31–32; 13:41; 25:31–32). Though it may sometimes mean just 'I', more often it is a veiled reference to himself as the **Messiah**, and influenced by Da 7:13–14 where 'one like a son of man' is vindicated by God.

SOUL A word with a rich variety of meaning in both the OT and NT. Basically it means 'possessing life' (Ge 2:7; 9:4; Lev 17:10–14; Ro 11:3; 16:4). Also refers to that from which physical appetite arises (Nu 21:5; Dt 12:15; 20–24) and emotions come (Job 30:25; Ps 86:4). Further, it is the source of the will and moral action (Dt 4:29; Ps 24:4; 25:1). Thus **salvation** of the soul (Heb 10:29; 1 Pe 1:10–11) is of the whole person. Soul and body are not distinguished in the Bible as they are in Greek philosophy.

SPIRIT The human spirit is that invisible breath which is the source of life (Ps 31:5; 51:17; 142:3–4). The Spirit of God is the invisible power of God active in the world and within individuals. In the OT the Spirit of God is said to inspire prophets (Eze 11:5; Pr 1:23; Isa 59:21), and charismatic judges (Jdg 3:10; 6:34; 11:29; 14:6), to pervade the natural order (Ge 1:2; Ps 139:7) and to be responsible for marvellous things (Joel 2:28–29). In the NT the Holy Spirit is particularly associated with Jesus whom he anoints, fills, guides and empowers (Lk 4:18ff; Mt 12:28). Then after the resurrection of Jesus the same Spirit comes to the Church from the Father through the Lord Jesus (Ac 2:1ff; Ro 8:11ff; Gal 5:18ff) to continue his work in and through believers. See **Holy Spirit**.

STEPHEN (crown). The first Christian martyr (Ac 6–7), stoned to death by the Jews. Chosen by the apostles as one of the Seven (Ac 6:1–6) to supervise the practical charity of the Church, he was also a preacher and full of faith, grace, wisdom and spiritual power (Ac 6:5, 8, 10). He was granted a vision of the exalted Lord Jesus in heaven (Ac 7:55–56).

STONE Apart from its use in buildings, stone was used for weapons (1 Sa 17:50), weights (Lev 19:36), knives (Ex 4:25), landmarks (2 Sa 20:8), writing tablets (2 Co 3:7) and as **pillars** (Ge 28:18; Dt 27:5). Jesus is figuratively called a stone (Mk 12:1–11, cf Ps 118:22; Ac 4:11; 1 Pe 2:4ff).

STONING The usual form of execution for **Hebrews** was stoning (Ex 19:13; Lev 20:27; Lk 20:6; Ac 7:58). Prosecution witnesses had to throw the first stones (Dt 13:9f; Jn 8:7).

SUFFERING God made the world good, without suffering (Ge 1:31), and the new universe will also be without suffering (Rev 21:4; Isa 65:17ff). Suffering is associated with the disturbance caused by **sin** (Ge 3:15–19) and **Satan** (2 Co 12:7; Job 1:12; 2:6). It affects people everywhere, but only to the degree that God allows it to do so (Am 3:6; Isa 45:7; Mt 26:39; Ac 2:23). Suffering is always a problem to believers (Hab 2:2–4; Ps 73) even though they know that Christ will deliver them from all suffering, corruption and death (Ro 8:21; 1 Co 15:26). Its effects can be good—purifying the **heart** (1 Pe 1:7; Ro 5:3), bringing a closer relationship with God (Ro 8:35–37) and a sense of sharing in the sufferings of Christ (2 Co 1:5ff; Mk 10:39; Ro 8:17).

SYNAGOGUE (place of assembly). The Jewish meeting place found in all parts of the Mediterranean world in NT times (Lk 12:11; 21:12; Ac 17:2). The local centre for Jewish worship, education and government (Lk 4:16; Mk 5:22; Ac 13:15; 18:8).

SYRIA See page 42.

TABERNACLE The portable sanctuary/tent shrine built by Moses for Israelite worship as a result of the **covenant** the LORD made with Israel at Sinai (Ex 25:40; 26–27; 35–38; 40:34). Inside were the altar of burnt-offering, the laver and the Tabernacle proper (= the **Holy Place** and the **Most Holy Place**). In the latter was the **Ark** of the Covenant (Ex 25:16, 22; Heb 9:4). After entering Canaan it was kept at **Shiloh** (Jos 18:1), Nob (1 Sa 21) and Gibeon (1 Ch 16:39) before being replaced by the **Temple** of Jerusalem. See also **Tent of Meeting**.

TABERNACLES, FEAST OF Known as the festival of **Booths** (Lev 23:34; Dt 16:13) and of ingathering of harvest (Ex 23:16; 34:22) it was a compulsory, pilgrim festival (Ex 23:14–17; 34:23; Dt 16:16). Israelites were required to live in booths/tabernacles made of branches (Lev 23:42).

TAMAR (palm). (1) The wife of Er and Onan (Ge 38:6ff). (2) A daughter of **David** (2 Sa 13:1ff). (3) A daughter of Absalom (2 Sa 14:27). (4) A city of SE Judah (Eze 47:19; 48:28).

TARSHISH (1) A grandson of **Benjamin** (1 Ch 7:10). (2) A prince of Persia (Est 1:14). (3) Son of Javan and grandson of **Moah** (Ge 10:4; 1 Ch 1:7), and also referring to his descendants and the land they occupied—probably near the **Red Sea** (1 Ki 10:22; 22:48; 1 Ch 7:10; Jnh 1:3; 4:2).

TARSUS An ancient city of Cilicia, situated by the river Cydnus and about 10 miles inland from the coast of Asia Minor. The birthplace of the apostle **Paul** (Ac 9:11; 21:39).

TEACHERS OF THE LAW See **scribes**.

TEMPLE Although reference is made to the temples of various deities (Jdg 16:26) the interest of the Bible is in the three successive temples in Jerusalem. See page 46.

TEMPTATION AND TESTING In God's providence, people are tested by him; in this testing he may use the temptations of Satan. God places people in situations which test their faith or commitment (Ge 22:1; Ex 16:4; 1 Co 3:13). **Satan** tempts them seeking to lead them away from doing God's will (Job 1:12; 2:6; Mt 4:1–11). Temptation is not **sin**, but yielding to it is sin (Heb 4:15; Jas 1:2ff; 1 Pe 5:10). Testing by God makes a person stronger in faith, hope and love (1 Co 3:10–15).

Believers are also to test the spirits—to learn to distinguish between the actions and presence of the **Holy Spirit** and the deeds and power of evil spirits (1 Th 5:21; 1 Jn 4:1).

TEN COMMANDMENTS Spoken by the heavenly voice from Mount **Sinai** in the hearing of the tribes of Israel and twice written down by the 'finger of God' on both sides of two tablets of stone (Ex 19:16–20:17; 25:16; 31:18; 32:15–16, 19; 34:1, 28; 40:20; Dt 5:6–21). They represent the essence of the **covenant** that God made with **Israel**.

TENT OF MEETING Either the small provisional meeting-place of God in use before the larger Tabernacle was built (Ex 33:7–11) or the actual Tabernacle itself (built according to divine instructions). See **Tabernacle**. The provisional Tent of Meeting was pitched outside the camp and upon it the cloud of glory descended: the Tabernacle was pitched in the centre of the camp and the cloud of glory went into it (Ex 40:34–35).

TETRARCH A Roman ruler of an Oriental province of the Empire. The noun is only used of Herod Antipas in the NT (Mt 14:1; Lk 3:19; 9:7; Ac 13:1).

***THADDAEUS* Disciple** and **apostle** of Jesus (Mt 10:3; Mk 3:18). Also known as Judas son of James (Lk 6:16).

THEOPHILUS (friend of God). The man to whom Luke dedicated both parts of his two volume work, Luke and Acts (Lk 1:3; Ac 1:1). His identity is unknown.

THESSALONICA Named after Thessalonike, sister of Alexander the Great, and became the principal city of Macedonia. It was situated on the great trade routes from Italy to the East and from the Aegean to the Danube. **Paul** evangelised here and wrote two letters to the church there (found in the NT)—Ac 17:1–9; 1 & 2 Th.

THOMAS (twin). One of the twelve **apostles** (Mt 10:2–4; Mk 3:16–19). Personal references to him only come in the Gospel of John—11:16; 14:5; 20:24, 26, 28.

THYATIRA A city in the west of modern Asiatic Turkey, an important point in the Roman road system for the province of **Asia**. The church here received a Letter from John (Rev 2:18–29).

TIBERIAS A city on the western shore of the Sea of **Galilee** and named after the Emperor Tiberius (Jn 6:23: cf Jn 6:1; 21:1).

TIBNI A short-lived king of Israel (1 Ki 16:21–22).

TIGLATH-PILESER III King of Assyria 745–727 B.C. He invaded Israel in the reign of Pekah (2 Ki 15:29–30) and took gifts from Ahaz of Judah (2 Ki 16:7ff).

TIMOTHY (worshipping God). Companion and assistant of **Paul**: of a Jewish-Christian mother and Greek father

(Ac 16:1–3; 17:13–15; 1 Co 4:17). Two letters to him from Paul are in the NT (1 & 2 Ti).

TITHE(S) The tenth part devoted to God. The **Law** of Moses required that a tenth part of the yearly grain, wine and oil as well as the firstlings of the flocks and herds be given to the **Levites** and **priests** (Dt 14:22f; 2 Ch 31:5; Neh 10:38; Mal 3:10).

TITUS A convert, friend and helper of **Paul**, whose name is not mentioned in the Acts but to whom Paul wrote a letter which is in the NT. He is mentioned in 2 Cor 2:13; 7:6, 13, 14; 8:6, 16, 17, 23; 12:18; Gal 2:1, 3; 2 Ti 4:10.

TOBIAH (Yahweh is good). (1) A deputy of Sanballat (governor of Samaria) who opposed the work of Nehemiah in Jerusalem (Ne 2:10f; 6:18f; 13:4f). (2) A family who returned to Jerusalem from exile in Babylon but could not prove that it was authentically Jewish (Ezr 2:59–60; Ne 7:61–62).

TONGUES, GIFT OF A spiritual gift of the **Holy Spirit** by which believers are enabled to praise God in ecstatic speech (Ac 2:1–13; 10:44–46; 19:6; 1 Co 12–14).

TRADITION Teaching handed down from a teacher to his disciples. In Jewish circles this meant commentary on the Scriptures given by **rabbis** and **elders**. Jesus believed that the commentary often ran contrary to the real meaning of the text (Mk 7:3f).

TRANSFIGURATION, THE It was probably on Mount Hermon that Jesus' face and clothing shone with heavenly brightness as **Moses** and **Elijah** talked with him (Mt 17:1–8; Mk 9:2–8; Lk 9:28–36). The disciples **Peter**, **James** and **John** witnessed this remarkable event.

TRIBES OF ISRAEL When Israel entered Canaan led by Joshua it did so as twelve tribes. They had descended from

the twelve sons of Jacob (Ge 49) and a portion of the land
was allocated to each (Jos 13:1ff). Tribal distinctions mat-
tered until the period of Exile: but with the return under
Ezra and Nehemiah they became of little significance:
being a Jew was what counted.

TRUMPETS, THE DAY OF BLOWING OF A festival day
(Nu 29:1; Lev 23:24) to commemorate the beginning of the
civil year: trumpets and horns were blown all day.

TRUST In both OT and NT believers are urged and
encouraged to rely upon, have confidence in and commit
themselves to the LORD for he alone is trustworthy (Ps
37:3, 5; 40:3–6; Pr 16:20; Jn 14:1; Ac 14:23; Ro 10:11;
15:13).

TRUTH That which is consistent, faithful and dependable.
So God himself is truth (Ps 57:3; 96:13) and Jesus is truth
personified (Jn 14:6; Eph 4:21). As truth from God the
Christian faith is truth (Gal 2:5; Eph 1:13) and disciples are
to live within this truth (Jn 8:44; Jas 1:18) in the strength of
the **Holy Spirit** (Jn 16:13; 1 Jn 4:6).

TURN Used often in both OT and NT of turning to God in
penitence/repentance/trust/faith (Dt 30:10; Isa 55:7; Eze
33:11; Ac 26:18, 20) and of God himself turning from
planning wrath to sending blessing upon his people (Ps 6:4;
119:36; Am 1:3-13; Ac 7:42).

TYRE The main seaport on the coast of Phoenicia, where
the river Litani enters the sea. **Solomon** had many dealings
with the king and city (1 Ki 5:1; 7:13–14) and Jesus visited
the area (Mt 15:21–28; Mk 7:24–31). Christians were there
(Ac 21:3–6).

UNCLEAN The OT distinguishes between spiritual/moral
uncleanness and ceremonial/religious uncleanness (Lev
5:2f; 7:19f; Jn 18:28). Concerning the latter, certain animals were unclean (Lev 11), people became unclean on

touching a dead body (Nu 19) or catching skin disease (Lev 13ff) or when fluid (e.g. blood) came from their bodies (Lev 15). See **clean**.

UNLEAVENED BREAD, THE FEAST OF Closely connected to the **Passover**, beginning on the day after it and lasting seven days (Lev 23:5–8). Bread made without fermented dough (= yeast/leaven) was eaten to recall the experience of being delivered from Egypt under Moses.

UR OF THE CHALDEES The city from which Terah and **Abraham** left to go to Haran (Ge 11:28, 31). It is probably the modern Tell el-Muqavyar in S Iraq by the river Euphrates.

URIM AND THUMMIM Small objects belonging to the **ephod** of the **high priest** which were placed in his breastpiece. They were next to his heart when he went in before the Lord in the inner **sanctuary**. On his exit they were probably thrown like dice and their fall revealed the divine will for the nation (Ex 28:30; Lev 8:8; Nu 27:21; Dt 33:8; 1 Sa 28:6; Ezr 2:63; Ne 7:65).

UZZIAH (Yahweh is my strength). Tenth king of Judah (767–740 B.C.) also called **Azariah** (2 Ki 14:21; 2 Ch 25:27–26:1). He extended the borders of Judah but was struck with leprosy (2 Ch 26:16–23).

VINE, VINEYARD The hilly regions of Canaan were used for vine growing; a vineyard was usually surrounded by a protective wall or hedge (Ps 80:8–13; Pr 24:30–31; Isa 5:5). Grapes were an important part of the diet—for raisin cakes (1 Sa 25:18), sugar and wine. Used by Jesus as a picture of himself and disciples (Jn 15).

VISION A message from God given as that which the recipient (prophet/seer) 'sees' vividly with the mind (Ge 15:1; Eze 1:1; Da 2:19; Ob 1; Lk 1:22; Ac 9:10; 16:10).

VOW A voluntary promise to God to perform some service which is pleasing to him (Ge 28:20–22; Lev 27:2, 8; Nu 30; Jdg 11:30; Ac 18:18; 21:23).

WAR Like all activity in Israel war had religious significance. Priests went with the soldiers (Dt 20:1–4; 2 Ch 13:12–16) and sacrifices were offered before battles (1 Sa 7:8–10; 13:19; 14:37; 23:2). The picture of battle is used to describe the final triumph of Christ over **Satan** (Rev 16:14–16; 17:14; 19:14).

WAVE-OFFERING In connection with certain sacrifices a part of the animal or crop (cereal etc) was waved physically before the Lord and that which had been waved went to the **priests** (Lev 7:30; 8:29; 9:21; 10:15; 14:12).

WEEKS, FEAST OF See **Pentecost**.

WINE AND STRONG DRINK The juice of the grape was normally red and plentiful (Dt 7:13; Ps 4:7; Pr 3:10). It was used as fresh juice, must (sweet wine) straight from the wine press, as wine after fermentation and as vinegar (Nu 6:3; Mt 27:48). A light wine, mixed with water, was part of the staple diet (Mk 2:22). It could also act as a medicine (1 Ti 5:23). 'Strong drink' was made from the juice of other fruit—dates, honey and barley. There are warnings about drinking to excess (1 Ti 3:8; Pr 20:1).

WISDOM In the OT the ability to form, put into operation and complete a particular plan. Thus **Joshua** (Dt 34:9), **David** (2 Sa 14:20) and **Solomon** (1 Ki 3:9, 12; 4:29ff) were wise. Wisdom in everyday life springs from reverence for the LORD and is his gift (Job 28:28; Ps 111:10; Pr 1:7; 9:10). This is because God alone is truly wise (Job 12:13ff; Isa 31:2; Da 2:20–23). Jesus matured in wisdom (Lk 2:40, 52; Mt 13:54; Mk 6:2) and became the personification of wisdom (Pr 8:22ff; Mt 11:19; Lk 11:49; 1 Co 1:24, 30).

WORD OF GOD In OT times the spoken word of the

prophet was held to have a particular, dynamic quality
(Isa 55:10–11; Ps 119:89). Thus the word of God is the
source of the created order (Ge 1:3), the origin of the call to
service (Isa 6) and the content of the prophetic message
(Jer 1:2–13; 1 Ki 18:1; Eze 6:1). Even when written down it
held its power (1 Pe 1:25). In the NT the word is the gospel
of the **kingdom of God** (Lk 5:1; Ac 4:31; 2 Co 2:17): further,
Jesus is the Word made flesh (Jn 1:1) who also speaks the
word of the Father (Jn 17:14, 17). The word of God and the
Spirit of God work together (Heb 4:12).

WORKS (1) God's acts and deeds on behalf of **Israel** (Dt
3:24; Ps 46:8; 64:9). (2) The acts and deeds of Jesus as
Messiah (Mt 11:2–5; Jn 5:36; 9:3–4; 10:37–38). (3) The
acts and deeds of believers, done out of love of God (Eph
2:10). (4) The acts and deeds of those who (wrongly) seek
to gain God's favour by their efforts in doing what is right
(Eph 2:9; Ro 3–4; 11:6).

WORLD Sometimes used in a neutral sense of either the
universe as created order or of the world of human beings
(Ge 11:9; Ac 17:24). However, in the NT it often refers to
the world of human beings as in a state of rebellion against
its Creator, in the grip of evil forces and dominated by pride
and covetousness (Ro 3:19; 1 Co 1:20; Eph 2:2; 1 Pe 2:11;
1 Jn 2:15–17; 4:1–17; 5:4–19). Christ comes into this world
of sin in order to be the Saviour of people there (Jn 3:16ff;
1 Jn 4:14); the **Holy Spirit** convinces this world of its sin (Jn
16:8ff); believers are to be in this world but not of its spirit
(Gal 6:14; 1 Jn 2:15) for this world itself is to be totally
renewed (Rev 11:15).

WORSHIP In the OT God is specifically honoured by
thanksgiving and praise at specific shrines—e.g. the movable **Tabernacle** and the **Temple** of Jerusalem. **Sacrifice** of
animals was an important part of this worship: but in the
synagogue the worship was without sacrifices. Israel was to
worship God as LORD and him alone (Ex 20:5; 23:25;
34:14; cf Mt 4:9–10). In the NT worship may still be in

Temple and synagogue but the churches meet in houses and apart from the Lord's Supper have little ritual (Ac 20:7; 1 Co 16:2; 11:18–34). Christ's **resurrection** makes the worship of the Temple obsolete (Heb 3ff).

YAHWEH (or Jehovah). The Hebrew name for God, usually rendered LORD in modern English translations. See **LORD**.

ZACCHAEUS A chief tax-collector who entertained Jesus and became his disciple (Lk 19:2–8).

ZADOK (righteous). The name of six men in the OT chiefly of the priest in the time of David (2 Sa 8:17) who helped to bring the **Ark** into Jerusalem (2 Sa 15:24–29). **Solomon** made him high priest (1 Ki 2:26–35).

ZEALOT A member of a Jewish patriotic group, formed to resist the Roman aggression. A disciple of Jesus called **Simon** had been a zealot (Mt 10:4; Mk 3:18; Lk 6:15; Ac 1:13).

ZEBULUN (habitation). The tenth son of **Jacob**; his mother was Leah (Ge 30:19–20). His descendants (Ge 46:14) became a tribe of Israel (Nu 1:31; 2:7) who settled between the Sea of **Galilee** and the Mediterranean (cf Mt 4:12–16 & Isa 9:1–2).

ZECHARIAH (Yahweh remembers). The name of thirty men in the OT/NT but chiefly of (1) The fourteenth king of Israel, the last member of the dynasty of **Jehu** 753–752 B.C. (2 Ki 15:8–12). (2) The prophet (Zech 1:1, 7) who returned to Jerusalem from Babylon and whose oracles form the Book of Zechariah. (3) The father of **John the Baptist** who served as a **priest** in Jerusalem (Lk 1:5–67).

ZEDEKIAH (Yahweh is righteous). The name of five men in the OT but chiefly of the twenty-first and last king of

Judah (597–587 B.C.) who was placed on the throne by **Nebuchadnezzar** (2 Ki 24:18–25:7; 2 Ch 36:11–14).

ZEPHANIAH (hidden of the Lord). The name of four men in the OT but chiefly of the prophet whose oracles form the Book of Zephaniah. He ministered in the early part of **Josiah**'s reign (Zep 1:1, 8).

ZERUBBABEL (shoot of Babylon). Grandson of Jehoiachin (Ezr 3:2; Hag 1:1). Possibly the same person as Sheshbazzar, who was appointed governor of his native land by **Cyrus** (Ezr 1:8, 11; 5:14) and on returning to Jerusalem from Babylon rebuilt the **Temple** in 520 B.C. (Ezr 6:16–22).

ZIMRI The name of five men in the OT but chiefly of the fifth king of Israel 885–884 B.C. (1 Ki 16:9–20; 1 Ch 8:36). His reign was short, wicked and inglorious.

ZION One of the hills upon which Jerusalem was built (2 Sa 5:6–9), captured by David. He brought the **Ark** here and made the hill sacred (2 Sa 6:10–12). Later Zion was used of the whole of the 'holy city' of **Jerusalem** (2 Ki 19:21; Ps 48; 69:35; 133:3; Isa 1:8).

ZIPPORAH Daughter of Jethro/Reuel, the priest of Midian, and first wife of **Moses** (Ex 2:21). Mother of Gershom and Eliezer (Ex 18:1–6).

THE NIV STUDY BIBLE

General Editor: Dr Kenneth Barker

The NIV Study Bible is a comprehensive one-volume combination of the Bible text with helpful notes, maps and references. Nearly fifty contributors, most of whom were NIV translators, have sought to share their knowledge of the background and literary structure of Scripture, and to explain and clarify theological issues.

Features include 20,000 study notes which explain words and concepts, interpret difficult verses and give textual and historical background, introductions and outlines to every book in the Bible, 100,000 cross references in a convenient central column and 100 maps and charts placed throughout the text. A short concordance and subject index are also included.

'A superlative volume . . .' *Baptist Times*

'Of all the study Bibles available this must be the best . . . a treasure trove' *Restoration*

The NIV Study Bible is available in hardback and leather bindings.

THE HODDER AND STOUGHTON ILLUSTRATED BIBLE DICTIONARY

General Editor: Herbert Lockyer

Who were the Philistines? What is the theme of the Epistle of James? What does the Bible say about the Holy Spirit? This completely new compilation provides the answer to these and thousands of other questions, in a book that is easy to use and understand, designed with the needs of general readers in mind. Features include 500 full colour illustrations, 5,500 up-to-date entries, outlines of each book in the Bible, balanced articles on key theological subjects, biographical sketches of biblical characters and a colour map section.

The Hodder and Stoughton Illustrated Bible Dictionary was compiled by a team of five editors and eighty contributors representing respected evangelical scholarship.

THE NIV HANDY CONCORDANCE

Edited by Edward W. Goodrick
and John R. Kohlenberger III

The NIV Handy Concordance is a thorough and comprehensive guide to the New International Version. It may be used to locate and trace biblical references to verses, to identify occurrences of a particular name or place, to study parallel passages, in fact all forms of Bible study will be quicker and more accurate with this concordance as an aid.

Special entries are included for 260 Bible characters, with descriptive phrases and references summarising key events in that person's life. An additional feature is the listing of 44 familiar Authorised Version words, cross referenced to their NIV equivalents.